Tradition and the Founding Fathers

Tradition
and the Founding Fathers

Louis B. Wright

University Press of Virginia
Charlottesville

This title in the Monticello Monograph Series
is published with the support of
the Thomas Jefferson Memorial Foundation.

THE UNIVERSITY PRESS OF VIRGINIA
Copyright © 1975 Thomas Jefferson Memorial Foundation

First published 1975

Chapter II was read at the annual meeting of the Virginia
Historical Society on January 21, 1974, and published in
The Virginia Magazine of History and Biography 82 (April
1974): 131–43. Chapter III was given at the annual meeting of the United States Capitol Historical Society, September 27, 1972, and printed in the *Congressional Record* for
October 4, 1972. Chapter IV was prepared for the Twelfth
Annual Keese Lecture on March 28, 1973, at the University
of Tennessee at Chattanooga. Chapter V is adapted from
lectures first given at the Rushton Foundation at Birmingham, Alabama, in 1954, but modified for presentation before
the Anglo-American Historical Conference in London in
1965. Chapter VI was read at the Oregon Shakespearean
Festival, Ashland, Oregon, on August 15, 1972. Chapter
VII is adapted from *Essays in Honor of David Lyall Pat-
rick* (Tucson: University of Arizona, copyright 1971), pp.
45–67. Chapter VIII was read at the meeting of the Classical Association of the Atlantic States, Carlisle, Pennsylvania, October 27, 1972. Chapter IX was prepared for the
annual meeting of the American Council on Education,
Denver, Colorado, October 11, 1968. Chapter X, presented
on the occasion of the Tenth Cosmos Club Award, March
26, 1973, was first privately printed by the Cosmos Club,
copyright 1973, Cosmos Club, Washington, D.C. Chapter
XI was given on July 4, 1974, at Monticello for the Thomas
Jefferson Memorial Foundation.

Library of Congress Cataloging in Publication Data
Wright, Louis Booker, 1899–
    Tradition and the Founding Fathers.
    1. United States—Intellectual life—Addresses,
essays, lectures.   I. Title.   E169.1.W83   917.3′03′2
74–23551   ISBN 0–8139–0621–0

Printed in the United States of America

Contents

Foreword

THE CONTINENTAL CONGRESS in Philadelphia having on July 2, 1776, adopted the resolution of independence from Great Britain, John Adams on the third wrote home to his wife: "The Second Day of July, 1776, will be the most memorable Epocha in the History of America—I am apt to believe that it will be celebrated, by succeeding Generations, as the great anniversary Festival. It ought to be commemorated, as the Day of Deliverance by solemn Acts of Devotion to God Almighty. It ought to be solemnized with Pomp and Parade, with Shews, Games, Sports, Guns, Bells, Bonfires and Illuminations from one End of this Continent to the other from this Time forward forever more." Independence has indeed been commemorated and solemnized, as John Adams predicted, for nearly two centuries, but on July 4, when twelve states agreed to the written Declaration embodying the resolution. The Fourth of July became the occasion for pomp and parade, shows, games, sports, and the like, and especially political oratory, throughout the United States.

At Monticello, the home of the author of the Declaration of Independence, the day has an especial poignancy, for Thomas Jefferson died there on the fiftieth anniversary of the great event. The Thomas Jefferson Memorial Foundation has annually arranged a Fourth of July observance in front of the east portico of Monticello. It is a good country festivity, strongly reminiscent of nineteenth-century celebrations. Crowds of people mill about in extreme heat, seeking the shade of trees. A token of "pomp and parade" is provided by the colorfully uniformed Monticello Guards and the Charlottesville Municipal Band. Boy and Girl Scouts and the American Legion lend their hands in the observance. To add seriousness to the occasion a federal judge convenes the

United States District Court, Western District of Virginia, for naturalization ceremonies, while the Albemarle Chapter, Daughters of the American Revolution, presents American flags to the new citizens.

No Fourth of July anywhere is considered complete without speech-making; normally this is a perquisite of holders of public office, the higher the better. But in the spring of 1974 many Americans had less confidence than usual in the integrity of their government. The vice-president of the United States had taken leave unexpectedly only a few months before. The president himself, hanging desperately to the ropes, was within a few weeks of leaving the ring. Even when one applied to the twentieth-century United States government the twenty-sixth of the sixteenth-century Anglican Articles of Religion – "Of the Unworthiness of the Ministers, which hinders not the effect of the Sacraments" – July 4, 1974, did not seem the ideal moment to listen to holders of public office. Consequently the 198th anniversary of the Declaration and the 148th of the death of Thomas Jefferson seemed a desirable time to ask a distinguished historian to give the address at Monticello.

Dr. Louis Booker Wright, Director Emeritus of the Folger Shakespeare Library in Washington, came to Monticello to deliver an address entitled "The Obligation of Intellectuals to Be Intelligent: Some Commentary from Jefferson and Adams," which is the last chapter in the present volume. An old-fashioned humanist, Louis Wright has resisted current tendencies toward specialization, by which many scholars write more and more about less and less. In *Louis B. Wright: A Bibliography and an Appreciation*, published by the University Press of Virginia in 1968 when he retired from the Folger Library, it was noted: "Ordinarily even the most distinguished scholar's bibliography is simple enough to compile and to arrange. What he has written falls within fairly narrow limits of specialization, the number of items to be listed is relatively small, and the whole is easily manageable. But when the scholar is Louis B. Wright, ordinary rules cease to apply. Equally expert in literature and history (whether English or American) Mr. Wright's intensive study of the past has never excluded lively interest and concern with the present and the future. The 314 items of this bibliography reflect a mind which refuses to be bound by time, place, or subject."

Louis Wright is a scholar whose broad learning is made especially palatable by a sense of humor and a vividly pungent literary style. His comments on matters of present-day concern are unforgettable, for he does not suffer fools with the gladness enjoined by St. Paul. Moreover, to borrow an expression from my friend Elliott Perkins, he "can tell mud from molasses at a hundred and fifty yards. He does, too, and tells the bystanders." The numerous addresses that he gives contain so much of permanent value that they should be readily available to a wide group of readers who will profit from his wisdom and wit. Consequently the Thomas Jefferson Memorial Foundation and the University Press of Virginia sought permission to publish a selection of his addresses, including the one delivered at Monticello in 1974.

Of the eleven chapters in this book, seven are published here for the first time. Nine have been written since 1971; the two that were prepared earlier were never published. Consequently the contents of this book represent writings not listed in the 1968 bibliography. The general subject—tradition and the founding fathers—makes the work particularly appropriate reading for the year 1975.

As I read the essays of Louis B. Wright, I am inevitably reminded of a commencement address given at Georgetown University in 1959 by another man with the same family name, then Bishop of Pittsburgh, now His Eminence John Cardinal Wright, Prefect of the Sacred Congregation for the Clergy in Vatican City. Cardinal Wright included a spirited section on the value of leisure, the advantages of a sense of humor, and the important place of mere nonsense in human life. "One wonders," he said,

whether a saving sense of humor would not provide as much as almost anything else, save only the Faith, that perspective needed to correct some of the grim extremes of our sometimes overly earnest educational and professional work. There is a deadly earnestness surrounding the discussion of the current problem of the intellectual life of America and the intellectual life of the Catholic church, a deadly earnestness which suggests that knowledge and information may be on the increase and wisdom and understanding on the way out. Education that leaves no time for nonsense is no education at all. In many books on American education which are flooding the markets presently one common note cuts across all differences of progressivism, conservatism, liberalism, aristocracy, classicism, and scientism. It is the appalling absence of any trace whatever of a sense of humor.

Although both these learned and like-minded Wrights have been valued friends of mine for more than a quarter of a century, I doubt that they have ever met, for their careers have followed different courses. Louis Booker Wright, whom I came to know on the council of the Institute of Early American History and Culture at Williamsburg, Virginia, is a South Carolinian, born in 1899, who attended Wofford College in Spartanburg, South Carolina, and the University of North Carolina at Chapel Hill. John Joseph Wright, whom I first knew when we served together on the Examining Committee of the Boston Public Library, is a Bostonian, born in 1909, who studied at Boston College, St. John's Seminary in Brighton, and the Gregorian University in Rome. Indeed, the only similarity visible in the pages of *Who's Who* is that each holds twenty or more honorary doctorates from universities here and abroad. The elder spent his active career at the Huntington and Folger libraries; the younger has been Auxiliary Bishop of Boston, Bishop of Worcester, Bishop of Pittsburgh, and since 1969 the only American member of the Roman Curia.

The similar turn of mind of the two Wrights comes, I suspect, from their early schooling. Louis Wright gave an engaging account of his childhood in the "Dark Corner" of South Carolina in *Barefoot in Arcadia, Memories of a More Innocent Era*, published in 1974 by the University of South Carolina Press. There we learn that not only his schoolmaster father, Thomas Fleming Wright, but his family in general, "being classically inclined, brooked no skepticism about the value of Latin and Roman literature." John Wright was educated at the Boston Latin School, founded in 1635, which in his day still preserved a strict classical curriculum. Speaking in 1960 at a dinner commemorating the 325th anniversary of the school, he observed: "The Latin School taught and teaches that wisdom, as against the fancies of the progressive education fans who, in their folly, encourage young people to express themselves before they have anything to express. This was the blessed wisdom behind Latin School customs that made us keep bottled up our unripened wisdom until it could somehow season and mature. Hence the happy pain by which Latin School required of us *declamations* before we were encouraged to debate, forcing us to stock our minds with the lofty concepts of our elders and to taste on our lips the words of our betters before we presumed to trumpet our own small thoughts."

In *Barefoot in Arcadia*, Louis Wright offers a chapter entitled "Education by Osmosis and Observation," which begins:

"The learning process"—a term bandied on the tongues of countless pedagogues nowadays—is varied and devious, and, like smallpox vaccination, sometimes takes and sometimes doesn't. Although a horde of Americans, male and female, derive a livelihood from pondering its mystery and publishing opaque views in pedagogical journals, the taming of young barbarians remains a problem fruitful of speculation and controversy.

Hardly a week passes without some educational medicine man shouting the virtues of a new panacea that will ease the pain of learning, cure all the ailments of the schools, and turn loose upon the land a generation of youngsters smarter than their elders. Though prophets flourish like crabgrass in June and bewilder the public with doctrines and prescriptions, the older generation remains convinced that youth is going to hell in a hurry— at an enormous increase in school taxes. The educational system, like dandruff or falling hair, remains unsolved. Some get educated and some don't. That is what happened in less sophisticated days and is what probably will continue to happen until the end of time.

Most education is inadvertent. Children learn by observation, imitation, and accidental influences. If they are lucky, their parents subtly—or maybe not so subtly—will see that they stumble over useful influences.

Barefoot in Arcadia makes it clear how Louis Wright acquired "an early addiction to reading" through an abundance of books. The classical inclinations of his family, and the constant reading of the King James Bible, caused the "learning process"—dreadful phrase—to "take" for all time. That is what might be expected in a rural area settled in the eighteenth century by Ulster Scots—"Presbyterians with a conviction that they were called of God to smite the heathen and to occupy the land."

The learned tradition of Scotland is strong in the writings of Louis Wright, a fact gracefully recognized in that country when he became an honorary doctor of the University of St. Andrews in 1961. It is worth noting that Cardinal Wright is also a Scot. His great-great-grandfather, Fraser Wright, a native of Edinburgh, was in the glass business, which he moved to England. His great-grandfather for whom he is named, John Joseph Wright, came from England to Boston in 1852. If one dug back far enough in Scottish records, one might discover that the two Wrights are ninth cousins. Such investigation is needless, however, for they are brothers in spirit, who exemplify the Horatian adage: "Quamquam ridentem dicere verum quid vetat?"

The following eleventh-century rhymed hexameters were written by Reginald of Canterbury, a native of Poitou who became a monk at St. Augustine's, Canterbury, about 1090. Although they are part of a long poem in honor of the Syrian hermit, St. Malchus, they apply with equal appropriateness nine centuries later to Louis B. Wright or, for that matter, to the cardinal, who first called them to my attention two decades ago.

> *Te posuit lumen sapientia, dans tibi flumen*
> *Quo flueres vivo felix septemplice rivo;*
> *Nempe tuo vivi septem de pectore rivi*
> *Insimul emanant qui languida pectora sanant.*

Foreword

Et cibus est menti doctrina tui documenti
Palladis ad cenam cupienti scandere plenam.
Tu iam duxque viae, tu fons splendorque sophiae
Monstrans namque viam cupidus potare sophiam.

Wisdom holds you up as a light, granting you eloquence
Wherewith, in sevenfold stream, you happily gleam;
From your heart seven living rivers flow
Curing the hearts of the languid.
The knowledge of your wares is a food for the mind,
    a banquet
For one desiring to approach the full table of
    knowledge.
You are a guide, and a leader on the way,
You are a fount, and the splendor of wisdom
Lighting the path before those desirous of devouring
    wisdom.

WALTER MUIR WHITEHILL
President, Thomas Jefferson
Memorial Foundation

Tradition and the Founding Fathers

I

Belief in the Value of the Past

IN OUR TIME it has been fashionable in certain intellectual quarters to decry any adherence to tradition as inhibiting and detrimental to social and spiritual freedom. Too long society has been bound by the fetters of the past, this doctrine proclaims. We must free ourselves from the bondage of inherited beliefs and concepts transmitted to later generations by historians who themselves were befuddled by ancient myths having little validity in the past and no "relevance" for the present. By word or implication youth is warned to disregard the croakings of the ancients in their midst. The elders of the tribe, it has been discovered, no longer are repositories of wisdom, or even of knowledge, and youth would discover "truth" best by exploring its own ego.

Our ancestors who lacked the benefits of instant communication and instant information from the ends of the earth were so old-fashioned that they still believed in the value of an inherited body of traditional knowledge. The founding fathers of the Republic looked back to Greece and Rome for guidance and wisdom. They believed that from history and great literature, especially the history and literature of the classical world, they could profit from the accumulated experience of humankind. From childhood, these men had also been taught to respect the sagacity that experience and the mellowing of time brought to the older members of society. They had not yet learned that teenagers should be listened to with awe. On occasion they were heard to voice the heresy that children should be seen but not heard.

The founding fathers, for all their concern to establish a republic that would guarantee freedom under law to its citizens, were even more concerned to safeguard the new nation from the social chaos of anarchy. They all believed in dis-

1

cipline and the exercise of authority to maintain social stability. Not even the most liberal of them would have condoned the permissiveness advocated by many advanced thinkers today.

The doctrines of Jean Jacques Rousseau, already attracting attention among some of the "enlightened" of the eighteenth century, would have to wait for several generations to gain wide acceptance in the United States. Few if any of the founding fathers, not even an idealist like Thomas Jefferson, could stomach Rousseau's doctrine of the noble savage or his insistence that children should be permitted to grow and unfold without restraint or prohibition. These beliefs, so objectionable to the founding fathers, had to wait until our generation to gain widespread acceptance, supported by the dicta of educational psychologists and specialists in pedagogy.

Education, our unenlightened ancestors believed, required among other things the mastery of certain well-defined bodies of traditional knowledge. Higher learning meant the study of Latin and Greek, sometimes even Hebrew. William Byrd II of Westover in Virginia, for example, noted in his diary throughout his life constant reading of Latin, Greek, and Hebrew lest he grow rusty in these languages and be unable to enjoy the substance of the literature in those tongues.

Present-day educationists have pointed out the folly of such concepts. In *News of Amherst College* for March 1973 the lead paragraph announced the abandonment of any foreign language requirement for a degree at Amherst and explained: "Since most other traditional degree requirements no longer persist, many members of the faculty found it indefensible to maintain what they considered a vestige of the past. The only degree prerequisites remaining are in the number of courses successfully completed, four years of residence (and in unusual cases this can be reduced), departmental major requirements, the comprehensive examination, and certain prescribed activities in the Department of Physical Education."

Instead of wasting a student's time nowadays with slaving over the mastery of a foreign tongue, much less one of the "dead" languages, we have substituted live and relevant courses in "communication," one of the most popular subjects in colleges today. In some institutions a student can major in communications and, if he so elects, graduate with a panoply of techniques on how to be a television announcer—blue or striped shirt, the latest in necktie design, hair just the fashionable length, voice modulated—and advice on how to give instant analysis of any item in the news. Instant communication has become the obsession of our generation, and the media cater to and encourage it.

The "right to know" has also suddenly become the right to invade any man's privacy, to take pictures of his dying wife if "newsworthy," and to harass any public official or private citizen. All of this would have astounded Thomas Jefferson, who more than once declared that he had given up reading newspapers in favor of Tacitus and other classical authors.

The men who created the Republic were profoundly concerned with current events of their day and the implications of happenings for themselves and for society. But they did not require quick answers to all questions. They were willing to wait until all evidence obtainable was in hand, and then they expected to meditate upon an event before jumping to a hasty conclusion. No reporter hastened to a television camera on July 4, 1776, to explain to tense Americans what this revolutionary statement would mean to them, interspersed, let's say, with commercials for the sale of Benjamin Franklin's improved stoves or his fire-preventing lightning rods. The public of 1776 had to wait for an announcement in the various weekly gazettes and draw their own conclusions about how the Declaration would affect their lives.

Few traditional beliefs had a greater impact on eighteenth-century Americans and the generations that came after them than what is popularly called the "Puritan work ethic." This doctrine was not exclusively Puritan but was the accepted doctrine of every social group. Martin Luther had discussed

3

the problem of one's calling and had asserted that every man —and woman—must labor in whatever calling God had placed him. A similar assertion was made by a famous Elizabethan preacher, William Perkins, widely read in America, who wrote *A Treatise of the Vocations* (1603), explaining the necessity of work for all mankind. Drones were intolerable in any well-ordered society; not only were the indolent to be refused support from charity, but they would be required by law to labor at some vocation.

This doctrine, voiced by countless preachers, came to be associated with the Puritans. The most influential advocate of the so-called Puritan work ethic was not a preacher at all but that most worldly-wise of Americans, Benjamin Franklin. The advice on work and thrift that Franklin heard in his youth in Boston, reinforced by the common sense and thrift of Quaker ideas in Philadelphia, gave him a background of bourgeois philosophy which he expressed in the sayings of Poor Richard and in his *Autobiography*.

Franklin and all the other founders of the nation would have been enormously troubled had they foreseen a day when the work ethic, like many other things they accepted as unalterable truth, would be called in question, even ridiculed as a belief that had outworn its time. Of late, social theorists have been busy convincing themselves—and anyone else whom they can convert—that blue-collar workers, even white-collar workers, are all discontented, that work itself is wicked, that the summum bonum is leisure. The use that men and women will make of their leisure is an unresolved problem. One notable thinker recently announced that they must have time to "pursue happiness," with the implication that this pursuit means the elimination of stultifying labor of any description.

If it has occurred to such observers of man's estate that even yet many people find profound pleasure and satisfaction in work well done, these wise men of Gotham have given no evidence of that discovery. To them work appears to be a burden thrust upon us, probably by the sin of Adam. Had he not eaten of that apple we might all be lolling around

Eden gently brushing flies from our naked torsos. So widespread has become the worry about the wickedness of work that *U.S. News and World Report* for July 29, 1974, printed a four-page interview with a psychiatrist, Dr. Saul M. Siegel, described as "an expert on Workaholics." In this interview, entitled "If You Think You Are Working Too Hard," Dr. Siegel observes that some millions of people are addicted to overwork, but he points out that we know too little about this condition: "The condition is not seen as a problem because whatever remnants of the Protestant work ethic are left in our society encourage us to look up to people who work hard." When we have rooted out the last remnants of this heinous work ethic, many more millions will realize that they have been working too hard. They can then seek out a psychiatrist—or get themselves on the burgeoning welfare rolls and relax. We have made a hopeful beginning with some thousands of hippies soaking up sunshine in some of the pleasant spots on the planet; but they must never stray too far from a post office where they can expect a check from the folks back home to save them from the iniquity of the despised bourgeois work ethic that victimized poor old dad.

The creators of our nation had another antique quality that has come to seem a bit quaint to some of our contemporaries: a premium that they placed on gentility and good manners. Nearly every man of prominence and standing aspired to be a gentleman. Today of course such aspirations are liable to get a man ticketed as class-conscious and undemocratic. An exhibition of good manners, especially in the young, is proof of a lack of "sincerity" and the honest revelation of one's feelings.

The "in thing" for a young man nowadays who wants to be "with it" is to avoid any display of manners: to push ahead of everyone through any door, trample on as many toes as possible, never step aside for a "lady" (a tabooed word) lest he be accused of male chauvinism, and exchange jolly four-letter obscenities over cocktails with any female in sight, who is expected to respond in kind. Such behavior would have offended the least cultivated of the founding fathers. Indeed, some of them might have been moved to horsewhip youths who so violated their sense of decency and decorum.

The eighteenth century, which saw the beginning of our nation, had many faults. The men who labored over its creation were not perfect; they made many mistakes. But they all had a sense of being part of a great enterprise, and they did the best they could. Because most of them were men of property, economic determinists have tried to show that the Constitution was primarily designed to protect the property rights of the well-to-do. It seems never to have occurred to these theorists that men have sometimes been able to rise above selfish interests to act for the public good. Whatever mistakes the founding fathers made, whatever faults they displayed, they acted for the public interest as they perceived it. Men like Adams, Jefferson, Franklin, Madison, and many others believed that privilege carried with it an obligation of responsibility. Their views and their actions are worthy of continued study. Perhaps some students of this bygone age and these bygone manners may be vouchsafed the grace of imitation.

II

Tribulations of a New Nation

HISTORY MAY NOT repeat itself, but similar conditions do repeat, and historians continue to hope, perhaps vainly, that we can learn from past experiences of the race. But because we make the same mistakes over and over again, historians are liable to show a spirit of pessimism.

The trouble is that human nature is static, perverse, and given to sin and error. The Puritans of the seventeenth century believed that only divine mercy might save a remnant of humankind from the abyss of depravity. Although since that time great phalanxes of missionaries have labored in the vineyard of the Lord, armies of apostles of progress have assured us of the perfectibility of mankind, and whole squadrons of do-gooders have earnestly proclaimed the elimination of poverty or some other panacea as the way to bring about the millennium, we continue to wallow in misery, iniquity, and crime. Only in certain material developments does society show progress: in medicine and the relief of pain, in the more effective production and distribution of food, and in the increase of physical comfort generally. I once heard a debate: "Resolved that aspirin has brought more joy to mankind than wine and whisky."

Pessimists viewing present-day society sometimes like to refer to the "good old days" that never were. A realistic view of our past history shows that from the beginning we have been subject to many of the sorrows, political and social, that still afflict us. These may be attributed to the incorrigible nature of human beings. In America we have had an enduring element of idealism, manifest in every period, but that idealism has resulted in little genuine improvement in the quality of our civilization. Indeed, some cynics have maintained that the idealists have caused more misery and unhappiness than

7

all the rascals. I once heard a Bostonian assert that his city enjoyed better government under Mayor Curley, who at one time was reelected while serving a jail sentence, than it had under its idealistic reform mayors. Under Curley, he claimed, stealing was controlled and restricted to a select few, while under virtuous dreamers, thievery in public office was rampant. As to that, I have no special knowledge.

What I would like to do now is to review very briefly some of the problems that beset our ancestors as they tried to establish a new nation. They were not unlike us in their varied political, social, and economic views, their mistakes, their shortsightedness, or their dreams, aspirations, and idealisms.

We must remember that in 1776 the country's leaders had declared their independence of colonialism and had established a republic, the first government of its kind since the republic of early Rome. For the Venetian state, though it might call itself a republic, was not a democratic government, nor were the little Swiss cantons parallel to the new government that our founding fathers created from their knowledge of classical history and literature.

The new American Republic was acclaimed by its creators as a model that other peoples, oppressed by tyrants, might follow. At once we began to assert the desirability of exporting our system to other countries, an insistence that has become an article of faith with Americans. From 1787 onward, we have rarely paused to question whether the American Constitution and the American ballot box would suit Italians, Portuguese, Africans, Samoans, or Vietnamese. We have convinced ourselves that we know what is good for other people, namely, our form of so-called democracy. That belief and our missionary instinct for purveying it have cost us enormous sums in national wealth and great loss of life, revealing a persistent naïveté in a people who have failed to catch a glimmer of ethnic and political reality through the centuries.

Early in our history we were nearly swept off our feet by enthusiasm for the French when they overthrew their king,

Louis XVI, cut off his head, and established a sister republic. Surely this was proof that our example was being followed and that we were setting a pattern that would induce the oppressed of the world to overthrow all tyrants and usher in an era of justice to the common man.

Before the French populace dramatically ended royal rule with the guillotine in 1793, an action widely approved in the new United States, we had spent seventeen difficult years trying to launch our own ship of state. To a consideration of those troubled years I want to return in a moment, but first I would like to describe the hysterical fervor with which we greeted the news that the French had followed our example in warring against tyranny. We demonstrated in 1792 and 1793 a faith in the export of our political ideals that has plagued us—and the world—ever since.

In December 1792, when word came that the coalition armies attacking the new French government were in retreat, celebrations broke out all over the United States. Typical was a dinner held on December 20 in Baltimore, at "Mr. Grant's Fountain Inn." There, it was reported, "a numerous and respectable company of gentlemen, Friends of the Rights of Man," met to celebrate "the late triumph of liberty over despotism in France." After "partaking of an excellent dinner" they drank "fifteen republican toasts." The drinking of gargantuan quantities of punch characterized celebrations of the overthrow of despotism. Enthusiasm for the French Revolution reached a frenzied climax at a vast "Civic feast" held in Boston on January 24, 1793. Local newspapers whipped up excitement for days preceding the event. When the great day came, citizens of all ranks marched in parade. An array of butchers in white smocks holding knives and cleavers strode ahead of a wagon bearing a whole roast ox, carts loaded with bread, and still more carts with hogsheads of punch. From the left horn of the ox floated the republican flag of France, the flag of the United States from the right. Tables set up in State Street were piled with meat and bread, and flagons of punch were free to all comers. Soon Boston glowed with an incendiary fire for revolution and the destruction of all despots. That afternoon another procession marched from the statehouse to Faneuil Hall, where Sam Adams presided over a banquet. More toasts were drunk to liberty and the rights of man. So fervent was human sympathy for the downtrodden that someone persuaded authorities to release all prisoners from the town jail so they could "join their festive brethren and again breathe the air of liberty," as one newspaper reported.

Similar celebrations, equally convivial, were held throughout the country. At a banquet in Philadelphia after the beheading of Louis XVI, a barbecued pig, symbolizing the late king of France, was brought in. Its head was cut off and passed around the tables as each guest, "placing the cap of liberty upon his head, pronounced the word 'Tyrant,' and proceeded to mangle with his knife the head of the luckless creature."

So ardent was the enthusiasm for all things French that men and women believed, as one toast proclaimed, that the world was soon to be "one great democratic society comprehending the human race." A Bostonian expressed the hope and belief that all distinctions, even of language and nationality, would disappear as the Rights of Man described by Tom Paine prevailed.

For a time the cult of revolutionary France was so strong that enthusiasts exhorted their brother Americans to give up all titles, even *Mr.* and *Mrs.*, and substitute *Citizen* and *Citess*. [Cf. *Ms.*]. A social note in a Watertown, Mass., newspaper announced the marriage of "Citizen Frederick Geyer to Citess Rebecca Frazer." Any distinction, even between the sexes, was deplored by one citizen who suggested the use of the term *Biped* for all. Biped Jones would be married to Biped Smith.

At length the hysteria ran its course and Americans regained a modicum of sanity, but not before President Washington had been violently maligned for his proclamation of neutrality during the war between France and England. His political enemies led demonstrations against "government by proclamation" and demanded that the people control foreign policy. Just how this was to be done was not made clear, but advocates of the Rights of Man apparently thought government could be administered by a huge national town meeting at which every blacksmith and tinker would have an equal voice. Americans, it was loudly proclaimed, should rescue the oppressed and the needy in every land. Then universal equality and justice would prevail. This impossible dream has never wholly vanished.

But we must return to an earlier period to note the struggle within the separate portions of the United States as the country battled to gain something approaching national unity. The trials and tribulations of the new nation offered little basis for the exalted notions of mission that some enthusiasts for world revolution advocated.

The Second Continental Congress, which approved the Declaration of Independence, was not a legislative body but a convention selected to propose measures for meeting the crisis with the mother country. This Congress had not contemplated a formal break with Great Britain when it had first met on May 10, 1775, three weeks after the Massachusetts militia had engaged in a skirmish with the British at Lexington and Concord. A civil war had started, but the Congress was still hopeful of wringing concessions from Great Britain and patching up the disputes. Nevertheless this Congress decided that the militia at Lexington had acted in the interest of all, and the Congress gave its approval by appointing George Washington commander in chief of the forces defending the rights of the colonies.

The Second Continental Congress represented primarily a party, the Whigs, who opposed the encroachments of King George III and his Tory party. At this stage many citizens of the colonies, perhaps the majority, still regarded themselves as loyal to the king. Only gradually during the year that followed the fighting at Lexington did the American Whigs win enough support to bring about a complete break with Great Britain.

When a delegate from Virginia introduced into the Continental Congress the resolution that led to the Declaration of

Independence, he declared that "the colonies are, and of right ought to be, free and independent states." That is precisely what they became after the signing of the Declaration: in effect, thirteen little sovereign states, often jealous and suspicious of each other, frequently opposed to each other because of conflicting interests. The relation of the individual states to the central government to be established was a critical problem, not completely resolved until the fratricidal Civil War of 1861–65. Only after that struggle could the United States claim to be one nation indivisible. In 1776 each new-fledged state was self-consciously aware of its independent sovereignty and determined to maintain its autonomy. The necessity of pooling some part of its sovereignty, even in the interest of survival, was a decision hard to make.

Among the states, neither unity of opinion nor a common interest existed. Settlers of the thirteen colonies came of varied nationalities and religious and social beliefs. Pennsylvania, for example, the most polyglot of all the states, had many German sects, some of them pacifists, who wanted no part in a war of independence. The state's ruling group was dominated by English Quakers, most but not all of whom opposed an open conflict with Great Britain. On the frontiers of Pennsylvania were Ulster Scots, bitter over the way they had been treated by the English in Ireland. They were ready-made revolutionaries. But elsewhere, Scottish merchants and recently-arrived Highland Scots were loyal to the king's cause. In the towns many merchants who had argued most violently against the repressive acts of trade imposed by Parliament remained loyal to England when the break came. But not all merchants were loyalists. Some of the most patriotic American Whigs were prosperous merchants who ran the risk of losing everything in a war with Britain.

In recent years it has been fashionable to discover an economic motive behind political actions. Economic determinists have tried to show that the American Revolution was inspired by economic unrest, that the loyalists who remained true to the king were the prosperous and well-to-do, while the revolutionists were those who saw a chance of bettering their economic lots by changing the government. But economic motives were only partially responsible for the attitudes of the people in the crisis of 1776: individuals often took sides opposed to their economic interests. The American people, then as now, were a complex group, and facile generalizations about their motives and actions are likely to be wrong. In Virginia many of the great landowners stood beside backcountry frontiersmen in opposing Great Britain. Such men were Thomas Jefferson and Richard Henry Lee. In South Carolina rich merchants of Charleston opposed the king, while backcountry farmers remained loyal. Families were sometimes divided.

Religion played some part in the struggle, but the division along religious lines was not clear. Anglicans were generally conservative and many remained loyal. One of the great fears of American Dissenters had been that the Church of England would appoint an American bishop and attempt to strengthen the union between church and state. For that reason Congregationalists and Presbyterians were more anti-British than the Anglicans, but one finds many patriots among the Anglicans and many Tories among the Dissenters.

So wide were the differences among the American people that a realistic observer would have prophesied that they could never achieve national unity. Approximately one-third of the population remained loyalist, one-third was definitely in favor of independence, and one-third was neutral and tried to avoid taking sides. With this division it is almost incredible that the patriots could have waged a successful war of independence and finally established a nation strong enough to survive.

The first step toward national unity was the establishment of the semblance of a central government in the Articles of Confederation, which the Continental Congress drew up and accepted on November 15, 1777—more than a year after the colonies had declared their independence. Before it could be binding, each of the colonies had to ratify it, and this ratification was not complete until March 1, 1781, nearly five years after the Declaration of Independence! One of the reasons for the long delay was a controversy among the states over the disposition of western lands which several of the states claimed under their original charters. In the meantime, the patriots were waging a war against the British, with the Continental Congress serving as a sort of interim central government, but a government with no real power.

A pious historian once remarked that the American victory over the British was proof of divine intercession, for he could discern no other explanation. He might have added that the phenomenal incompetence of British leaders helped.

The selection of George Washington as commander in chief was one of the wisest steps the Continental Congress could have taken. Washington had had some experience as a field commander in the French and Indian Wars; he was no spit-and-polish officer and had little interest in the pomp and circumstance of military glory; he was a man of character and integrity; he enjoyed the trust of officers and men; he had a great deal of practical common sense; and he was tenacious and apparently undaunted in the darkest days of the war. Washington had need of all of these qualities, for as Tom Paine wrote after one bitter defeat, those were times which tried men's souls.

To a modern chief of staff Washington's task would have seemed utterly hopeless. He was commander in chief in name, but he found that he had to deal with fourteen more or less independent "armies"—if the small levies of untrained troops can be dignified by that term. The Continental Congress had authorized an army, and each of the states had an army of militia under state control. On request, the states might supply militia to supplement the troops of the Continental Army, but the states might keep the militia at home to protect their own borders. In South Carolina, for example, Tory bands in the backcountry were so strong that much of the fighting consisted of internecine guerrilla warfare between Tories and patriot militia units. States with powerful Indian tribes on their borders had to safeguard the outlying settlements against attack, for most Indians favored the British.

Modern staff officers who believe that campaigns are won by careful planning in logistics would have found Washington's military equipment and service of supply bad beyond belief. During the miserable winter of 1777–78 at Valley Forge, his men suffered for want of food, clothing, and fuel because he lacked both money to pay for supplies and transport to haul them. Rich farmers preferred to sell their meat and grain to the British, who could pay in gold; Washington could offer only the depreciated paper money.

Under so loose a command, discipline was hard to enforce. Officers themselves frequently wrangled and set a bad example by their disrespect for each other and sometimes by their drunkenness. Desertions were common. At times Washington's army almost disappeared as men went home without leave. A few of Washington's generals plotted against him and tried to replace him with another commander. Gradually, however, he acquired an effective fighting force.

One hope of the new American nation lay in gaining European allies. The best chance seemed to be the friendship of France and possibly of Spain. Astute Americans like Benjamin Franklin labored unceasingly to draw France into an alliance. At first France aided surreptitiously by supplying money while waiting to see whether the Americans themselves would display enough strength to warrant overt intervention. Finally, in February 1778, France and the United States signed a treaty of commerce and alliance, and in the following year Spain joined France in the war against Great Britain.

But these powers did not come to the aid of the infant republic out of altruistic sympathy. They came into the war for their own profit and in the hope of strengthening their imperial positions in the New World. The young United States was to be in almost as much danger from its allies as from its specified enemy.

The first French soldiers to aid the Americans were volun-

15

teers, adventurers who applied to Washington for commissions and expected preferential treatment in pay and rank. Most of the first-comers were more of a problem than a help. One of the few to prove his worth was Lafayette. The first French naval force under Admiral d'Estaing showed no zeal to fight. Not until Comte de Grasse replaced him did French sea power prove effective. Despite discouragements and defeats, American forces, reinforced by French aid, finally won a decisive victory at Yorktown in the spring of 1781.

Although some sporadic fighting occurred after Yorktown, the British surrender in effect ended the war. The American nation was actually free. It now faced the problems of peace, and, as so often happens, these problems were harder to solve than the more concrete problems of warfare.

During the years when the French were fighting beside the Americans and Spain was aiding France, both powers were planning methods of containing the new nation within restricted bounds. Spain was determined to prevent the United States from expanding beyond the Appalachians; France wanted a weak United States, one that would remain dependent and with which France could do business as with a colonial possession. To be saved from its friends was the United States' greatest need at the end of the war. To outwit these late "friends" and preserve a greater measure of territorial independence, the United States made a treaty with Great Britain without the consent of France or Spain, a treaty establishing the Mississippi as the western border of the nation.

During the early years of American independence the young nation had to make fundamental adjustments in its whole economy. In the long colonial period, the thirteen colonies had been, to a degree, tied to the mother country by economic bonds. New England had a larger measure of independence than any other section by reason of its shipbuilding, its fisheries, and its carrying trade; but even New England's trade, under the mercantilist regulations of the day, was carried on for the most part within the British Empire. The agricultural products of New York, Rhode Island, Pennsylvania, Maryland, Virginia, and the Carolinas found a market in England, whence they might be transshipped to other consumers. The tobacco merchants of Maryland and Virginia, the rice planters of South Carolina, the grain and meat producers of Pennsylvania, all depended on agents in London, Bristol, and Glasgow for markets and credit. They were dependent on their English agents in even more intimate ways. For example, the planters of the Chesapeake Bay area, a region virtually destitute of towns, expected their London factors to be purchasing agents for practically every item of use: a wedding gown for the planter's daughter, jewelry for his wife, a suit of clothes for himself, utensils for his kitchen, equipment for the farm, everything great and small that he needed. More than that, he sometimes sent his sons and daughters to school in England in the care of his factor and expected this industrious agent to report on their progress and serve in place of a parent.

Great Britain discouraged manufactures in the colonies. The home country would provide a market for raw materials, and the colonies would consume its manufactures. In theory both would flourish, but the mother country would flourish more.

The coming of the Revolution ended this imperial dream, and it also completely disrupted the pattern of life established over the years in all the colonies. The fear of such a disruption explains why many Americans preferred to remain loyal to the mother country. Readjustments seemed difficult if not, indeed, impossible.

Hardships were very great in the early years. Rice planters in the Deep South could find only a limited market; tobacco rotted in the fields and warehouses of Virginia and Maryland planters; New England merchants had trouble marketing their goods. American consumers of British goods went without customary supplies and were often in dire want.

Gradually, however, they made adjustments. Critical industries gained a foothold. Iron foundries, for example, flour-

17

ished in Pennsylvania and Maryland. By the end of the war the colonies were producing nearly enough fabrics for their needs. They found new markets for their produce. New England had long sold codfish in the Mediterranean countries. They now expanded their markets and developed trade with other countries.

The Dutch had for years carried on a considerable amount of contraband trade with the colonies. At the outbreak of the Revolution they supplied many of the products that had previously come from England. Dutch aid in the form of goods and credit helped the new nation make the transition to economic independence.

The political situation in the thirteen states during the early years of independence was chaotic. Unity of action was impossible. The Continental Congress, the only central agency of government, had no real legal power. It could not impose taxes, nor make laws, nor control the states in any way except by persuasion and influence. It could issue paper money, but it had so little support for this currency that its money quickly depreciated. Although Congress could make requisitions on the states, they might not comply, for Congress had no power to coerce any state.

Americans were afraid of central authority. Jefferson was to assert that the best government was the least government. Having experienced the British attempt to rule without regard for the people's wishes, Americans were fearful of another tyranny of their own creation. From time to time they were persuaded by Congress to take measures necessary to the conduct of the war, but they were not yet ready to enter into a social compact that delegated any of their sovereignty to an over-all authority.

The period when the country had for its only constitution the Articles of Confederation has often been described as an era of crisis, confusion, and chaos. John Fiske's *The Critical Period of American History, 1783–1789* (Boston, 1888), a book written with great literary charm, painted such a dark picture of conditions that his readers have difficulty believing that any constructive developments occurred. As a reaction against Fiske's point of view, Merrill Jensen's *The New Nation: A History of the United States during the Confederation, 1781–1789* (New York, 1950) emphasizes the progress made under the loose association of sovereign states, especially the achievement of economic independence.

But the Confederation, it is true, often appeared hardly a government at all. Its authority was weak, and it was by necessity inefficient. Yet despite its shortcomings, it provided a framework for the nation while a better system was being evolved.

A great debate was being waged long before the convention was called in 1787 to write a better constitution for the United States. This debate was taking place in thousands of informal as well as formal discussions, in newspapers, arguments among villagers, in the state legislatures, and wherever Americans with political interests congregated. The debate was over the question of how Americans would govern themselves now that King George was no longer their titular head. Much of the argument was naïve and much of it was pointless, but it showed an interest of the people in their own destiny.

Two widely differing points of view polarized. One group wanted a strong centralized government with authority over the states; the other group insisted on a retention by the states of their essential sovereignty. In the end, in 1787, when the American Constitution was adopted, the resultant document represented a compromise between extremes. It was what Catherine Drinker Bowen called it: a "miracle at Philadelphia."

The Constitution established a central authority with sufficient power, stated or implied, to govern with reasonable effectiveness in the national interest, and yet it left to the states the enforcement of most laws and the responsibility for the welfare of its citizens. The debate over the respective prerogatives of the federal and state governments, however, still goes on, and both major political parties have on occasion invoked "states' rights" as an issue when it has suited them.

Although the Americans had contrived to establish a republic, the weakness of the government and the wrangling of its citizens did not induce much optimism for the future. Realistic Europeans, surveying the little nation, showed little faith in its survival as an independent state. Many Englishmen believed that the United States would soon come knocking at the British Empire's door to escape being swallowed by one of the other world powers. France, of course, expected its ally to become a satellite. The internal problems were of such magnitude that many Americans themselves were doubtful about their own capacity to survive.

Conservative Americans were skeptical of democracy. Alexander Hamilton, first secretary of the treasury, is remembered unfavorably in liberal circles to this day for describing the people as "your great beast." Excessive enthusiasm in certain quarters for the dominance of the common man created a deep-seated fear among conservatives of a social upheaval that would destroy the framework of traditional society. Rabble-rousers like Sam Adams in New England did nothing to allay this worry. Tom Paine's *Rights of Man* was too revolutionary a dose for the conservatives to swallow, and the subsequent hysteria over the French Revolution, mentioned earlier, aroused doubts in the minds of even middle-of-the-road Americans. We can discern already the beginning of the great debate, not yet resolved, over the role of the common man in government. Extravagant statements in what would today be called leftist newspapers scared conservatives sometimes into extreme reaction. Later on, when Thomas Jefferson bought the Louisiana Territory in one of the greatest real-estate bargains of all time, many New Englanders strenuously objected to the introduction into the Republic of so many wild men from the West, especially Frenchmen of dubious political allegiance.

Yet despite all the fears, suspicions, and doubts in the minds of the new Americans, they managed to reach a compromise, not immutably perfect, but workable. They had a tremendous will to survive as an independent nation, and they were determined to grow strong enough to prevent any foreign power from encroaching upon that independent sovereignty.

Few nations have started so inauspiciously and under so many handicaps. But a small group of leaders of uncommon sagacity induced the majority to exercise mutual forbearance, tolerance, and plain common sense as they hammered out a viable instrument of government. Progress was never smooth, and the young nation's internal strains frequently appeared to foretell its doom. We have constantly trembled on the brink of a political precipice. Up to now we have managed to keep our footing and avoid slipping over.

Curiously, despite our visible shortcomings as a democratic state, we so often told ourselves that we were the best, strongest, and most virtuous of nations that we soon believed it. Europeans visiting our shores in the nineteenth century were amazed and appalled at our national conceit and vanity. With the growth of our good opinion of ourselves and the increase of our economic power came a concomitant increase in the sense of mission that we had manifested at the time of the French Revolution. We have profoundly believed in our obligation to convert other peoples to our form of government. We have also demonstrated an altruism in doing good by other peoples, according to our own lights—an altruistic generosity that has now left us financially bankrupt and spiritually exhausted.

In our zeal to reform other peoples, from Johannesburg to Kamchatka, we have allowed our preachments to outdistance our example. Our own governmental and social systems have been something less than perfect and require our eternal vigilance to keep them in even modest repair. Labor diligently as we may, we have been unable to alter traditional shortcomings of human nature. Greed, self-interest, and localism—which nearly wrecked our early plans to establish a government—continue to be dominant influences in politics, as they always will be. Only on rare occasions of great public danger are we able to rise above the demands of special interests. Affluence has been a particular hazard to the American people. We can avoid most perils more easily than those brought on by prosperity—and the fear of losing our material gains.

Historians, observing for generation after generation the ubiquity of our errors and the repeated collapse of our dreams, may be haunted by a certainty in their own minds that our efforts will be doomed to failure so long as human nature remains fallible. But that does not mean that we should retreat into negativism. We are obliged to espouse a philosophy of "as if." We must struggle onward, and we hope upward, *as if* success would some day crown our efforts. To do otherwise would be to confess defeat and drown in Bunyan's Slough of Despond. Intellectually we may suspect that we are not going to make the world any better, and that our own society will remain a moral desert, but we are obliged to retain an emotional dream that it will be otherwise. We have had that dream from the beginning, and we must live as if it might come true.

III

These Troublesome Commonwealths

TODAY WE HEAR constant lamentations over the divisiveness of American society, fractured among antagonistic groups. This divisiveness is attributed to ethnic differences, economic inequality, or regional separatism. Concomitant with the wailings over our divided social structure are calls for unity. One would think that we are facing a new crisis about to wreck the nation. Perhaps we should take comfort in looking back at our history. For we have always suffered from social tensions. Since these shores were first settled, every generation has complained of factions and conflicts of interest that threatened the peace of local communities as well as the good of larger political units. Dissension is the price we pay for democracy. Our system of government is very imperfect, but no one has managed to contrive a better one. The Greeks invented democracy and coined the word, but they never managed to achieve either harmony or unity under the system. We have actually come a long way since the days of Pericles, and we need not despair. Perfection, like infinity, can only be approached.

On August 24, 1972, the *Wall Street Journal* called attention to a current concept that is causing a certain amount of social unrest, the doctrine that we can achieve perfection in our governance if we have enough good will, or, conversely, that failure to solve the ills of society results from underlying corruption. Politicians have promised to end poverty, yet we still have millions on welfare; we continue to be plagued with crime, social evils, and war. Ergo, the Establishment must be callous, stupid, or wicked.

The dream of utopia, of the perfect state, has attracted the imaginative over the centuries, but it has always eluded mankind. No reformer has ever been successful in remodeling human nature. The Puritans practiced an ethic that emphasized diligence, sobriety, and thrift, but their constables had everlastingly to pursue the errant. Scriptural authority insists that the poor always we have with us, and the swelling welfare rolls attest to that Biblical truth. These are old conditions that go back to the beginning of history, our history and the history of everyone else.

Someone has explained the contemporary bitterness over our social ills by saying that what troubles youth (and others) is that now we have the resources for curing evil and yet we do not utilize the means at hand. But that thesis is questionable. It is debatable whether we have adequate ways of solving our problems. And the argument ignores the invincible perversity of human nature. The Calvinists evolved a doctrine of man's innate depravity; but even the eighteenth-century belief in the perfectibility of man did not entirely erase a lingering suspicion in many minds that maybe the Calvinists had hit on a truth. Lately, however, we have returned to the philosophy of Jean Jacques Rousseau and his concept of the noble savage. If only we are permissive, kind, gentle, soft-spoken, and free with our tax dollars, all will be right with the world, however red in tooth and claw. That belief of course has a discouraging history of frustration.

When we consider our historical background it is miraculous that we have succeeded in creating a relatively homogeneous society and a viable government. As Catherine Drinker Bowen called it, the Constitutional Convention of 1787 was, indeed, a "miracle at Philadelphia," for the colonies were all suspicious of one another, fearful of losing their individual sovereignties and determined not to fall victims to a powerful central authority. Rhode Island was so disinterested that it refused to send a representative to the convention, although thirteen merchants from Providence wrote expressing a hope that the "sister states" would not retaliate against Rhode Island for its lack of participation.

The moving spirits behind the convention did not dare assert that it was called to create a new form of government. Such news would have meant defeat before an opportunity arose for debating the issues. The Congress sitting in New York had authorized a "federal convention" "for the sole and express purpose of revising the Articles of Confederation." The states were asked to send delegates to Philadelphia for that purpose. But many suspected that more was afoot, and they were skeptical about any good that would come from such a gathering. The remarkable fact is that, between May and September, the delegates to this convention managed to hammer out a constitution that the states would eventually ratify, an instrument of government—with its subsequent amendments—under which we still live.

Even yet, we wonder how these men, differing so often in their backgrounds and points of view, suffering the tortures of a long, hot, Philadelphia summer, were brought to agree on so durable a document. If the result was a tribute to the spirit of compromise that a group of wise men induced, it also marked the culmination of 180 years of struggle to establish effective governance for English-speaking peoples on the North American continent.

At no earlier time had representatives of the various regions been able to agree on anything approaching unity. From the earliest days, even the smallest communities frequently had fallen to quarreling. From time to time the Board of Trade in London (which had authority over the colonies) or colonial statesmen themselves had suggested unity of action against outside forces or against Indian attacks, but rarely had colonies cooperated with each other. Jealousy or greed too often prevented any effective collaboration.

Quarrels that rent the little settlement of Jamestown during its first few years were symbolic of the rows that would break out in all the colonies. Capt. John Smith, whose strong hand saved Jamestown in several crises, barely escaped hanging at the hands of his colleagues. Three generations later, after surviving constant internal friction and disastrous Indian attacks, Virginia had a civil war: Nathaniel Bacon in 1676 rebelled against the government of Sir William Berkeley but died at the height of the uproar, and his forces melted away. Governor Berkeley wreaked such a terrible vengeance on his enemies that King Charles II grumbled that "the old fool has hanged more men in that naked country than I have for the murder of my father."

Across the Potomac, Maryland suffered an even more tempestuous sequence of disturbances than Virginia. Established as a proprietary colony granted to George Calvert, Lord Baltimore, and his family forever, it started as a haven for persecuted Catholics. Cecil Calvert wisely provided for religious toleration of all sects. This did not prevent Protestants from stirring up trouble. In 1654 a Puritan group, finding themselves strong enough, forced the Maryland Assembly to repeal the earlier and tolerant Act Concerning Religion and replace it with one forbidding freedom of worship to anyone believing in "popery or prelacy." Thus Maryland was beset with factionalism that continued for years.

The Puritan colonies to the north, for all their devotion to religion—even because of it—were all constantly racked by dissension. The pious brethren of Plymouth could not abide the pollution of their region by Thomas Morton, an Anglican who set up a maypole at Merry Mount (now Quincy, Massachusetts), invited Indian squaws to a dance, and otherwise profaned the place. To end these revels, Miles Standish (called by Morton "Captain Shrimp") marched to Merry Mount, arrested Morton, and shipped him off to England. This comic opera episode, however, was only a minor incident among many greater quarrels that disturbed the New England colonies. Massachusetts Bay exiled Roger Williams in the dead of winter for his religious views. Making his way through the snow to Narragansett Bay, Williams set up a colony in Rhode Island that sought to provide for religious freedom for all sects. His hope of avoiding faction was in vain, for human nature prevailed and the settlements of Rhode Island were constantly squabbling over land titles, boundaries, or something or other. It was said that "in the beginning Massachusetts had law but not liberty and Rhode Island had liberty but not law."

Massachusetts Bay, of course, dominated New England

but could not achieve peace within its own borders or with its neighbors. This colony's golden age was the period before the reign of Charles II, when the Puritan saints, led by such stalwarts as the Mathers, were virtually independent of authority from London. But in 1676 the Lords of Trade sent over an investigator, a conscientious and irascible fellow named Edward Randolph, a communicant of the Church of England, who made a report that found little good in Massachusetts Bay's Puritan regime. In 1684 the London authorities canceled Massachusetts' charter and made it a royal colony. Two years later a royal governor, Sir Edmund Andros, arrived with instructions to unify New England and extend his authority over the whole region. In the face of protracted war with the French and Indians, he was ordered in 1688 to add New York and New Jersey to his dominion. Thus the north had the appearance of a union that could face French power in Canada. Actually, unity existed only on paper. When the news reached the colonies of the Glorious Revolution of 1688 and the accession of William and Mary, New England rebelled against Andros and returned to its old independence and individuality.

The new government in England, however, still wanted unity in the northern colonies. In 1691 Richard Coote, first Earl of Bellomont, came over as governor of Massachusetts, New Hampshire, and New York, and military commander in time of war of Rhode Island, Connecticut, and New Jersey. Although Bellomont tried to bring about cooperation among the colonies, he failed. Quarreling groups feuded with each other and with the governor. Bellomont was unable to collect money or supplies needed for military protection against the Indians and the French. Like George Washington in a later day, he complained bitterly about the government's inability to raise money, to recruit troops, or to requisition even food for the fighting men.

One might think that greater harmony and a more Christian spirit of charity would have existed in Pennsylvania, founded by William Penn, a gentle, just, and fair-minded Quaker. But peace even in Pennsylvania proved a delusion, and that colony was the scene of constant bickering down to the Revolution and later. The fact that it was the most polyglot of the colonies may help to explain its problems, for its population consisted of English, Welsh, Scottish, Swiss, French, and German settlers of various religious beliefs. The Quakers and the early-arriving German Mennonites and related sects were pacifists; the Ulster Scots, who moved out to the frontier, were pugnacious and contentious. They incessantly complained about the failure of the Quaker government in Philadelphia to give them any help in fighting the Indians in the backcountry. The refusal of the pacifists, who for many years controlled the Pennsylvania Assembly, to do anything to protect the borderlands against the attacks of the French and Indians was regarded by others as a scandal.

By 1688 Pennsylvania had become so torn by disputes that Penn as proprietor and nominal governor sent over a former Cromwellian soldier, Capt. John Blackwell, to serve as deputy governor; Penn himself had to remain in England. The pacifists were bitter at having a soldier placed over them and made a great clamor, refused to cooperate with the deputy, and generally thwarted him at every point. Penn, upset by the contentions, urged his deputy to show tact, and wrote that he was "sorry at heart for your animosities . . . for the love of God, me, and the poor country, be not so governmentish, so noisy, and open in your dissatisfactions." After a year Blackwell begged to be relieved and shook the dust of Pennsylvania from his feet. On his departure he declared that the Philadelphia Quaker was a person who "prays for his neighbor on First Days and then preys upon him the other six."

Penn himself had realized that the future success of the colonies required unification, and in 1697 he drew up "A Plan of Union for the Colonies." This was one of many such suggestions made by men on both sides of the Atlantic in the period before the War of Independence, none of which ever succeeded. Penn the idealist in 1693 had also dreamed of universal peace, and during a stretch in Fleet Prison had written an "Essay toward the Present and Future Peace of Europe by the Establishment of a European Dyet, Parliament, or Estates." Colonial unity remained almost as elusive as peace in Europe.

Not only did Pennsylvanians quarrel among themselves, but the colony did not get on well with its neighbors. Penn had a long and bitter quarrel with Lord Baltimore over the boundary between Pennsylvania and Maryland. This dispute did not end until two English astronomers, Charles Mason and Jeremiah Dixon, between the years 1763 and 1767, surveyed and established the boundary between the two colonies, a boundary that became known, with larger implications, as the Mason and Dixon Line. The ruling Quakers in Philadelphia showed no brotherly love for their neighbors in the "Three Lower Counties," a region that after independence was to become the state of Delaware. The Philadelphians declared the people of future Delaware obnoxious and scorned "that Frenchified, Scotchified, Dutchified place," a scorn that the French, Scots, Dutch, and others of the Three Lower Counties bountifully returned. Amity was not a quality often discovered in colonial America.

Greed for land and greed for the advantages of trade, along with religious differences, accounted for much of the animosity. In South Carolina, for example, the low-country Anglicans showed little consideration for the up-country Scotch Presbyterians, who in turn despised the lowcountrymen. South Carolina Indian traders made long forays into the backcountry to deal with the Indians for deerskins and furs. This aroused the hostility of rival traders from Virginia. During Indian wars on the southern frontier, colonial governments had difficulty getting support from each other. The South Carolinians claimed that Virginia was glad to see them in trouble with the Indians or with the Spaniards or with anybody else who might diminish their competition for the lucrative Indian trade. During the savage Yemassee War (1715–18) South Carolinians charged that Governor Spotswood of Virginia, instead of sending aid to help his southern neighbor, was using the crisis to cement friendship with the Cherokees and other Indian tribes in order to steal trade away from South Carolina.

For some time the authorities in London had been aware that collaboration among the colonies was needed for mutual defense against the Indians, the French, or the Spaniards, as the case might be. Various proposals had been made, frequently by theorists who did not know colonial conditions at first hand.

In 1701 there was published in London *An Essay upon the Government of the English Plantations on the Continent of America . . . by an American*, a very rare but significant tract that I edited and published in 1945. The name of the "American" who wrote the tract remains unknown, but it may have been Robert Beverley or William Byrd of Virginia. From internal evidence it was certainly written by a Virginian who held views that Beverley and Byrd shared. An important portion of the *Essay* recommends a plan of union for the colonies that may have influenced later proposals for unification.

The immediate stimulus for the writing of the *Essay* was the publication in London in 1698 of a treatise by Charles Davenant entitled *Discourses on the Publick Revenues, and on the Trade of England. In Two Parts*. The second part of the treatise was enough to annoy any Virginian, for it stressed the value of the northern colonies to the detriment of Virginia, praised the pious thrift of the Puritan settlers to the north, commended William Penn and the proprietary system of administering colonies, and urged a plan of union for the colonies similar to the one submitted by Penn to the Board of Trade. Penn's plan recommended an intercolonial congress with equal representation from each colony. The meeting place would be New York, with the royal governor of New York serving as high commissioner and commander in chief. Virginia, then as later, could not agree to a proposal that gave the oldest colony, the one with the largest population, no more voice in affairs than the smallest province.

To refute Davenant's views, which echoed Penn's, and to utilize the opportunity to make many other suggestions for the better administration of the colonies (including the appointment of more competent royal governors) were the purposes of the *Essay*. The author agreed that a union of the several colonies might be desirable, but he insisted upon representation in a general assembly based on population and commercial importance. He also pointed out that it would be more fitting for the assembly to meet "sometimes in one province, and sometimes in another; and the chief governor in the province where they meet, being commissionated by his Majesty, may preside as commissioner in manner aforementioned." New York and its governor had no claim to be "advanced in dignity above the rest of the colonies," he declared. Finally he recommended a more equitable system of representation: "To obviate these and many other objections of this nature which may be made, it is humbly proposed that the whole continent be divided into five circuits or divisions thus: 1, Virginia; 2, Maryland; 3, Pennsylvania and the two Jerseys; 4, New York; 5, Boston, Connecticut, and Rhode Island; in each of which division let it be held by turns, one after another, in a certain order."

Charles Davenant, like other reformers from London, the author maintained, was a mere theoretician without adequate knowledge of the colonies; else he would not have glorified the proprietary colonies above the others. Ignorance of America by the authorities in England was the greatest unhappiness the colonies labored under, the author asserted.

Needless to say, nothing immediately came of the "American's" suggestions for unity and reform, though his views may have helped others later to mature their own ideas.

The most explicit effort to unify the colonies came in 1754 at the famous Albany Congress, where Benjamin Franklin set forth his celebrated Plan of Union. The colonies were facing a crisis that threatened colossal disaster. The French and Indian War (part of the conflict known in Europe as the Seven Years War) was beginning. France had succeeded in enlisting as allies powerful Indian nations; even the Iroquois, upon whom the English had depended for years, were being won over by French forest diplomats. In the light of news of deteriorating relations with the Indians, the Board of Trade in London had ordered the governor of New York to hold a council of Iroquois chiefs, to frame new treaties of friendship, and to call upon the other colonies to subscribe to these new treaties. This was the initial purpose of the Albany Congress.

Gov. James De Lancey of New York expanded the purpose of the congress to include discussion of unified action of the colonies to insure adequate defense and mutual cooperation. Benjamin Franklin, a representative from Pennsylvania, applied his fertile mind to the problem and came up with a proposal for unity. After lengthy debate the commissioners agreed that unification was necessary, and they recommended a provision for a congress in which the several colonies would be represented in proportion to population and importance. Only the Massachusetts delegates, however, had authority to sign any agreement at Albany; the others were not empowered to commit their respective provinces.

Some colonies had not even bothered to send commissioners. Because Governor Dinwiddie of Virginia had called a conference of chiefs of the Six Nations at Winchester, he did not think it necessary to participate in the meeting at Albany; Virginia preferred to go it alone. New Jersey replied that because it had never had any treaties with the Iroquois, the Albany meeting did not concern the colony. When the plan for joining into an effective union came up for consideration in the respective colonial assemblies, not one would agree to sacrifice a jot of sovereignty for the sake of union, even for mutual defense.

The idea of union was exceedingly slow to mature. Franklin's suggestions at Albany may have helped to induce the states, once independence had been declared, to consider articles of confederation. But even then individual states were too jealous of their sovereignty to surrender essential powers to a central government. With the former colonies at war with the mother country, it should have been abundantly clear to everyone that unity of action was necessary. Preceding the Albany Congress, Benjamin Franklin had printed his famous cartoon of a snake cut in pieces with the caption, "Join or Die." It was now republished, for never was cooperation more necessary.

Yet the Articles of Confederation, submitted to the Continental Congress in a first draft by John Dickinson on July 12, 1776, were not adopted until November 1777 and not ratified until 1781, when the Revolution was nearly over. Maryland for a long time had refused to ratify the Articles because its claims to western lands had not been settled satisfactorily. Other states were also disgruntled at various provisions.

Although the Articles proclaimed a "perpetual union," and provisions gave the central government authority to make war and peace, conduct foreign affairs, borrow money, raise an army, run a post office, regulate weights and measures, manage Indian affairs, and call upon the states for revenue and soldiers, yet the states would not surrender any rights of taxation or permit any coercion for failure to obey the central government's requests. In short, the government could only beg and express pious hopes that the states would show sweet reasonableness, tax themselves for federal benefit, and comply with other provisions of the Articles. Human nature being what it is, either individually or collectively, the Articles proved a very weak reed of government. Indeed, strong governments were feared. Radical propagandists opposed authority per se. Had not Tom Paine trumpeted in *Common Sense* that all governments (read today "the Establishment") are suspect and that "government, even in its best state, is but a necessary evil; in its worst, an intolerable one." In short, men should be wary of authority. This doctrine, lately rediscovered by long-haired youth and the apostles of the new permissiveness, has been bruited about as if it were something new.

The propagandists of the American Revolution, having picked King George III as arch-villain and catalogued his tyrannies in the Declaration of Independence, were concerned to emphasize the despotism of monarchy and all authoritarian rule. They succeeded too well. They convinced a large proportion of the populace, which needed little persuading, that strong governments are wicked. That propaganda, plus the natural inclination of the states to reserve all real power to themselves, thwarted General Washington's struggle to fight a war.

The low point in Washington's efforts to procure support from a powerless Congress and recalcitrant states came at Valley Forge because he had only Continental currency and little power to enforce the requisitioning of desperately needed supplies. The British, comfortably established in nearby Philadelphia, had plenty of hard money, and the farmers of Pennsylvania readily furnished them with beef, pork, wheat, poultry, eggs, butter, and produce of all sorts. In the meantime Washington's troops starved and froze. He wrote desperately to the governors of nearby states for help. To Gov. George Clinton of New York he described "the present dreadful situation of the army for want of provisions and the miserable prospects before us with respect to futurity. . . . For some days past there has been little less than famine in camp. A part of the army has been a week without any kind of flesh, and the rest three or four days." A New York colonel wrote to the governor: "I have upwards of seventy men unfit for duty only for want . . . of clothing, twenty of which have no breeches at all, so that they are obliged to take their blankets to cover their nakedness, and as many without a single shirt, stocking, or shoe, about thirty fit for duty, the rest sick or lame, and, God knows, it won't be long before they will all be laid up, as the poor fellows are obliged to fetch wood and water on their backs half a mile with bare legs in snow or mud" (George F. Scheer and Hugh F. Rankin, *Rebels and Redcoats* [New York, 1972] pp. 303–4).

How Washington won the war remains a mystery; perhaps it was another miracle like that in 1787 at Philadelphia; and, though it must not be said in derogation of the Father of Our Country, perhaps it was in part the stupidity of the

British high command. At any rate, Cornwallis surrendered at Yorktown, and the war was over. Then came the struggle to achieve a durable peace and to unify a country that only the threat of dire calamity had held together during the war. Once more the sections fell to quarreling.

When Chief Justice John Jay negotiated the Treaty of London in November 1794, it pleased nobody, for it made humiliating concessions to Great Britain. But on the whole it was better than a new outbreak of war. Washington used his influence to get it through the Senate, and it was ratified on June 25, 1795. "Peace," wrote Washington in defense of his position, "has been the order of the day with me since the disturbances in Europe first commenced." Yet the ratification of Jay's Treaty (as it was called) nearly split the country. Someone wrote: "Damn John Jay! Damn everyone who won't damn John Jay! Damn everyone who won't put out lights in his windows and sit up all night damning John Jay." Yet Jay's Treaty staved off a renewal of the conflict with Britain.

The early years of the new nation were filled with peril not only from outside enemies but from internal stresses. No European nation expected the Republic to last. Although the founding fathers looked back to the supposed virtues of republican Rome for a precedent, not everyone believed that a democratic republic offered hope of stability or even justice. Alexander Hamilton remarked in *The Federalist* (1788): "It is of great importance in a republic not only to guard against the oppression of its rulers but to guard one part of society against the injustice of the other part." Cynical Fisher Ames, contrasting monarchies and republics, commented: "A monarchy is a merchantman which sails well, but will sometimes strike a rock and go to the bottom; a republic is a raft which will never sink, but then your feet are always in the water." Not everyone agreed with Ames that the Republic would never sink. Jefferson wrote gloomily to his former secretary, William Short, then in Paris, that some conservatives were predicting the end of the Republic with the death of Washington.

The development of two political parties, the Republicans (later to become the Democrats) led by Jefferson, and the Federalists (much later to evolve into Republicans) led by Hamilton and others, soon resulted in violent and corrosive animosities. The French Revolution, coming so soon after the American War of Independence, was at first regarded as another glorious attack on tyranny and was toasted throughout America by enthusiastic supporters. But the French abolition of religion and the wholesale executions during the Reign of Terror produced a violent reaction among American conservatives. Because Jefferson had been an outspoken apologist for the French Revolution and was known to have abetted the revolutionaries when he was minister to France, he was characterized as a "Jacobin," the equivalent today of calling him a Communist. The Jeffersonians retorted by accusing Hamilton and the Federalists, who condemned the actions of the French, of being at heart pro-English and monarchists. The Republicans even claimed that the Federalists wanted to make Washington King George I of the United States and fasten an aristocratic government on the land. So the controversy raged, in pamphlets, newspapers, speeches, and in every tavern and public place. The hatred engendered nearly wrecked the Republic. Few presidential campaigns have ever been so bitter as that of 1800, which ended in the election of Jefferson.

What conclusions can we draw from so brief a survey of the rows, contentions, factions, jealousies, and suspicions that from the beginning divided the inhabitants of English North America? First we can take comfort in the knowledge that we are a reasonably durable political organism and not likely to collapse overnight. We might remember, however, a comment by Montesquieu in *The Spirit of the Laws* (1748): "Republics are brought to their ends by luxury; monarchies by poverty." Contemplation of that thought by social improvers might be fruitful.

Second, we can look back over history and remember that utopias have ever been a delusion, that the millennium is only a vague hope of mankind, that we are not likely to be

36

favored with perfection in individual or state, and that instant reform, instant social change, and instant solutions of our problems are merely a mirage seen by wishful thinkers.

Human nature remains relatively static, and no political nostrums are likely to purge us of short-sightedness, improvidence, laziness, selfishness, and greed. The Puritans tried to improve us by demanding sobriety, thrift, and diligence, but it is now fashionable to damn those qualities as bourgeois and benighted.

With mankind's previous efforts before us, we might maintain a cautious skepticism of the panaceas eagerly prescribed by professional sociologists. We might also seek to spare ourselves a flood of verbose advice from academia, a deluge of words from professors whose naïveté about the world around them is equalled only by their arrogance.

Third, the contemplation of history should leave us with at least a modicum of faith in the innate common sense of the majority of the populace. After all, we have swum to the surface through oceans of nonsense and survived.

We do not need to embrace the multitude with the enthusiasm of Jefferson, nor are we required to fear the judgment of the people with the doubts expressed by Alexander Hamilton. Lincoln's comment: "You can fool all the people some of the time, and some of the people all the time, but you cannot fool all the people all the time" is still sound political philosophy. No matter who promises what, we are not going to achieve perfection in our society or even approach it. That is reserved for the virtuous hereafter. Nevertheless, we must continue to struggle for the best that we have a right to hope for: that is, a balance in our political life between extremes. We should hope for wisdom to choose enough leaders with common sense to save us from the glittering dreams of well-intentioned idealists. Wise leadership in a republic is a rare quality. We would do well to pray for it and to remember the spirit of compromise that made possible the "miracle at Philadelphia" in 1787.

IV

The Middle-Class Tradition:
Legacy from Colonial America

FOR THE FIRST TIME in our history, the past decade has seen a small but vocal minority reject the bourgeois philosophy that has inspired millions of Americans in their struggle to improve their status and rise in the world. The term *middle class* has become a "naughty" word with many of the so-called intelligentsia who take pleasure in ridiculing the cult of success. Indeed, they contrive to give the impression that the effort to achieve financial independence, to acquire property and the essentials of comfort, is reprehensible. Barefoot philosophers sit around their communes scratching fleas, smoking pot, sipping apple wine, and railing at an Establishment that emphasizes thrift, sobriety, and diligence. This free and untrammeled communion with the ecology, uncontaminated by any zeal to labor, is, we are told, the ideal life for youth of this generation.

Blue-collar workers, a formidable report prepared by an official commission has informed us, are alienated and unhappy with their jobs on the production line. We must relieve them of the tedium that burdens their lives, for they are people without hope, mere automatons turning out cars or washing machines for a civilization that is spiritually bankrupt.

Further investigation, however, has revealed that the majority of blue-collar workers are not concerned with the ideology of the report writers. They do not consider themselves slaves of the production line. They draw top wages and are eager to keep their jobs. They are not generally frustrated, unhappy, or hopeless. On the contrary, they are buying second cars for their wives, taking vacations to go deepsea fishing off the Florida coast or engage in some other sport, and demonstrating the qualities of affluence that good jobs assure.

This is not to say that some blue-collar workers, like workers with any kind of collar, do not grumble. Grumbling about jobs is a normal condition of man—and woman—in any age and clime. Grumbling, however, is not proof of mass alienation or despair. The alleged condition of class discontent and frustration, in the opinion of some investigators, stems primarily from the beliefs and imaginations of theorists.

That many Americans are ready to throw overboard an ideology that has permeated our thinking since the colonial period is doubtful. From 1607 to the present moment, America has been a land of opportunity for the oppressed and the economically deprived peoples of other countries. Here, by hard work and thrift, they could get ahead and rise in the social scale. Social mobility has been one of our prized assets. Except for slaves during an earlier period, nobody was frozen into a class or caste. Although we endured the curse of slavery for many generations, emancipation came at last, and in modern times we have set about providing overdue opportunities for the black people of the nation. In this connection, it might be worth pointing out that human bondage was not a peculiarly American aberration, for throughout the world slavery of both whites and blacks was long condoned; for instance, not until late in the nineteenth century were the Russian serfs given their freedom. In the seventeenth and eighteenth centuries, the portion of North America that became the United States offered the individual greater opportunities to rise in the world than any other place on earth. We are still trying to improve those opportunities; only a small if clamorous minority seeks to reject this scheme of things.

Students of the continuity of the English tradition in America can find few more profitable veins to follow than the stream of bourgeois doctrine that has permeated Anglo-American thinking and writing since the founding of the colonies. If we are to comprehend the development of a tradition that has done more to shape American character, American thinking, and American aspirations than any other body of doctrine, we must go back to English writings of the sixteenth century.

Any effort to discuss the influence and quality of middle-class ideals is certain to result in oversimplification. Here I shall attempt merely to indicate tendencies that appear to me significant and to point out the wide acceptance of these doctrines of the marketplace.

We must remember that England in the sixteenth century underwent a transformation, from a country that was essentially agrarian into one that placed a new emphasis on trade, commerce, and industry. The change had been going on for generations. The wool trade with Flanders was older than Chaucer's time, and by Caxton's day Englishmen had learned some of the secrets of the Flemish weavers. But the sixteenth century, with its religious and political upheavals, its discoveries and exploitation of the New World, and its scientific innovations, was an era not unlike our own. The world grew infinitely complex, and the simple agricultural and grazing life, which had characterized England since before the days of Harold the Saxon, receded. The influx of gold and silver from Mexico and Peru—indirect as that importation was—brought about a creeping inflation that raised prices and helped to destroy fees and rents long established by custom. Landlords who found themselves undone were unaware of the forces that had ruined them. Tenants unable to eke out an existence on the soil where their forefathers had lived took to the road and drifted to towns and cities in search of work or charity. In certain areas industry flourished. The cloth business grew enormously. Huguenot and Walloon craftsmen, fleeing from persecution on the Continent, brought with them the secrets of their trades. London, Bristol, Norwich, Southampton, Plymouth, and other towns prospered. Merchantmen and buccaneers sailed from London or West Country ports to bring back the wealth of America, Asia, and the Spice Islands. A new class of citizens rose to power and influence: a commercial class of newly rich, men whose interests lay in trade and commerce, whose aspirations turned to pecuniary gain. These were the middle class, the capitalistic group destined to re-create England and to shape a new nation beyond the Western Sea.

The virus of gold, the infection with this fever germ of pecuniary profit, was no respecter of persons. It spread throughout the population. England in the late sixteenth and early seventeenth centuries became a land given to wild speculation. Bishops in their palaces, earls and dukes on their landed estates, merchants in their counting houses, apprentices, and yeoman farmers all heard about the profits to be made by subscribing to stock in a voyage to the East Indies or taking a share in some less savory enterprise. In the half-century between 1575 and 1625 England underwent a social change more far-reaching than any contemporary dreamed. An acceleration of commerce and industry took place in that fifty-year span that would slow down only during intervals of depression until its culmination in the Industrial Revolution. This social change—progress, if you like to call it that— profoundly influenced the spiritual and intellectual life of the nation.

Ethical standards, ideals of conduct and behavior, underwent a subtle modification, a change in emphasis rather than a transformation. An illustration of this shift of emphasis can be seen very clearly by studying Henry Peacham's *The Compleat Gentleman* (1622) and Richard Brathwaite's *The English Gentleman* (1630). Both books are intended to instruct a man in the proper education and behavior if he aspires to be a gentleman, an aristocrat. But from old-fashioned Peacham to new-fashioned Brathwaite, a world of change is evident. Country gentleman though he is, Brathwaite gives abundant evidence of the influence of the City, of the London of commerce, on his ethical and practical suggestions. These two books deserve careful analysis with a view to understanding their social significance.

By the beginning of the seventeenth century, timeworn ethical injunctions received a new polish and shone with

41

fresh glitter. Precepts designed to teach the prudential virtues became copybook texts. Young men learned that sobriety, diligence, and thrift were qualities that would lead to success—success meaning an accumulation of this world's goods.

We sometimes hear it said that the so-called ascetic virtues, these qualities of prudence, were a contribution of Puritanism, but that generalization is too easy. Ever since Max Weber's famous book on Puritanism and the Protestant ethic, we have heard that Calvinism was the parent of capitalism, but that generalization is also too easy.

English capitalism, it is true, received its first big impetus coincidentally with the rise of Protestantism, but capitalism would have developed if England had remained Catholic, as it did develop in Florence and Venice, for example, and in other Catholic regions. English Puritanism was congenial to many of the new commercial and industrial groups in England. London, the greatest commercial city in the kingdom, became a hotbed of Puritanism. The teachings of the Puritans appealed to the common sense of businessmen. They particularly liked the emphasis on "thou shalt not" doctrines, for did not young men, especially apprentices, need to be kept on the narrow path of duty? The iteration of the precepts to labor earnestly at one's task, to lead sober and frugal lives, and to save one's earnings against a rainy day or to provide the means for future investment occurs in countless Puritan manuals, but these injunctions are not *exclusively* Puritan. Church of England writers did not neglect them either. Their emphasis simply reflects the new middle-class mores. And one cannot say that the middle class begot the Puritans or the Puritans begot the middle class. They simply were a happy family together.

Diligent application to one's trade, a strict regard for sobriety at all times, and a thrifty concern to save every penny —the burden of much ethical advice in the manuals of behavior—left the apprentice little choice except to succeed. Success became his goal, a success frequently measured by the magnitude of his pecuniary gain. The gospel of success, made articulate in sixteenth- and seventeenth-century England, was brought to America and became one of the most conspicuous foundation stones of American society.

Many writers of all shades of theological opinion contributed their mite of ethical and practical advice, but few had a wider circulation on both sides of the Atlantic than William Perkins, Fellow of Christ Church, Cambridge, who died in 1602 in the bosom of the Church of England, though he had been known for his Puritan leanings. For more than a century after his death his works were prized in households in England, in New England, in Virginia, and in other American colonies. Scores of American inventories list "the works of Mr. Perkins," and many allusions in American writings attest his popularity and influence.

Perkins's teachings were practical and full of common sense. One need not expect in him any radical doctrines such as emanated from Anabaptists and other left-wing Protestants. His *Whole Treatise of the Cases of Conscience* (1606), a landmark in the development of Protestant casuistry, discusses, among many other social problems, the question of degree in society, and concludes that some men require more wealth than others and all men are not, and ought not be, of the same station. The law of nature, Perkins insists, "sets down and prescribes the distinctions of possessions, and propriety of lands and goods, and the Gospel doth not abolish the law of nature." He insists that poverty for its own sake is evil, smacking of popishness, and that charity, though commended to us all, should not be so indiscriminate as to encourage sloth. Upon the matter of taking interest he is explicit, pointing out that though men should lend occasionally to the poor without interest out of charity, it is just as proper to charge interest for money lent for investment as it would be to charge for the hire of a horse. Throughout his works, Perkins preaches a gospel of practical divinity, useful and not incompatible to the men of trade and commerce.

The most significant of his works for our discussion is "A Treatise of the Vocations, or, Callings of Men" (printed in his collected *Works* of 1603), one of the best statements of middle-class ethics from the Elizabethan period. It discusses both spiritual and temporal callings, themes found in much religious writing of the period. Perkins concentrates his major emphasis on problems of earning a livelihood. The most acceptable way of serving God, he insists, is by performing well one's everyday duties, and the surest way of attaining earthly happiness, as well as eternal salvation, is by laboring diligently in some honest trade or occupation. Honesty, thrift, diligence, and perseverance in one's ordinary pursuits are virtues to be prized and cultivated. Work is the handmaiden of morality and religion, and is desirable as an end in itself, albeit God in his wisdom has seen fit to reward the diligent with the fruits of his labor, and to punish the slothful with hardships and penury. Perkins's little treatise was the most explicit and detailed formulation of middle-class ethics before the publication of Richard Baxter's *A Christian Directory* in 1673.

Colonial Americans of varied religious beliefs used both Perkins and Baxter as practical guides to behavior. Cotton Mather in New England and William Byrd, Robert Carter, and other planters in Virginia found these two authors worth reading and retaining in their libraries.

Furthermore, both New Englanders and Virginians, to cite groups usually contrasted rather than compared, reflected much of the social doctrine found in these teachers of bourgeois ethics. The commercial society that developed in Massachusetts, Connecticut, and other parts of New England needs no description. The so-called cavalier society in Virginia is usually romanticized as the social opposite of the New England traders. Actually, there is much similarity in many of their social doctrines and attitudes. The Virginians, for example, suffered no nonsense about the taint of trade. That was a delusion which came with a period of decadence in the nineteenth century. One Virginia planter grew prosperous by baking ship's biscuit and selling them to the merchantmen plying the Virginia rivers. Robert Carter, the richest and grandest planter in colonial Virginia, was as diligent and earnest in his application to the multifarious business of his plantations, which included buying and selling, as any merchant prince of Boston.

But one hastens to add that the New England Puritans, being of somewhat sterner stuff in religion, contrived to make a rigid discipline of bourgeois ethics and to implement this discipline more thoroughly than their southern contemporaries. Nevertheless, let no one think that the social teachings of Perkins and Baxter were uncongenial to the Chesapeake Bay planters and their kind elsewhere.

It remained for a Boston-born resident of Philadelphia to epitomize the whole gospel of success and make it into a philosophy. That person, of course, was Benjamin Franklin, who knew Perkins and Baxter at first hand and certainly used Cotton Mather's adaptations of Perkins's doctrines. Franklin was the instrument by which most Americans, down to our own day, received the seventeenth-century adages designed to insure temporal success.

Many years ago, A. Whitney Griswold published a stimulating essay entitled "Three Puritans on Prosperity"—and listed Franklin as one of the Puritans.[1] One commentator on the essay asked somewhat querulously, "By what right Franklin is dubbed 'the soul of Puritanism'?" The evidence is clear to anyone who reads the Puritan preachers in the age preceding Franklin's. Moreover, Griswold showed that Franklin visited the aged Cotton Mather and modeled some of his first efforts in essay writing on Mather's work. The only complaint that one can make against Griswold's inclusion of Franklin among the Puritans is that the Puritans were not alone in their advocacy of the middle-class code of behavior. They simply did it more effectively than most others and provided the best discipline leading to material success.

The middle-class doctrines of seventeenth-century England, transmitted via Boston, reinforced by the common sense and thrift of Quaker ideas in Philadelphia, gave Franklin a background of bourgeois philosophy that he expressed most

[1] A. Whitney Griswold, "Three Puritans on Prosperity," *New England Quarterly* 7 (1934):475–93.

completely in the sayings of Poor Richard and in the *Auto-biography.*

The best epitome of Franklin's advice on how to get ahead in the world was compiled by himself in 1757 for the Almanac of 1758 and is known as "The Speech of Father Abraham," or by its more usual title, *The Way to Wealth.* Few if any other writings by an American have been so widely disseminated and so often quoted. Under the fiction of an old man delivering an impromptu bit of advice at an auction sale, Franklin gathered up his best proverbs and wove them into a fable full of sly humor and shrewd counsel. There, crystallized for all time, are adages that are still common-places in American thinking: "Early to bed and early to rise, Makes a man healthy, wealthy, and wise." "Industry need not wish." "At the working man's house, Hunger looks in but dares not enter." "God gives all things to Industry; then plough deep while sluggards sleep." "Sloth, like rust, consumes faster than labor wears; while the used key is always bright." "The sleeping fox catches no poultry." "Three removes is as bad as a fire." "Keep thy shop, and thy shop will keep thee." "A ploughman on his legs is higher than a gentleman on his knees." "Pride breakfasted with Plenty, dined with Poverty, and supped with Infamy." "The second vice is lying, the first is running into debt." " 'Tis hard for an empty meal bag to stand upright." These proverbs and many others in the same crisp idiom are a part of the little narrative of Father Abraham's speech, which warns near the end that "this doctrine, my friends, is Reason and Wisdom; but after all, do not depend too much upon your own Industry, and Frugality, and Prudence, though excellent things, for they all may be blasted without the blessing of Heaven; and therefore ask that blessing humbly, and be not uncharitable to those that at present seem to want it, but comfort them. Remember, Job suffered and was afterwards prosperous."

This little tract, which combined worldly prudence with a dash of piety, as a proper formula for success quickly gained an international audience. Franklin himself was astonished at, and not a little proud of, its reception. As he points out in the *Autobiography*, English newspapers printed it widely, householders bought broadside versions and stuck them up in their houses, the clergy and gentry distributed large quantities to their parishioners and tenants, and publishers in France brought out two translations. "In Pennsylvania, as it discouraged useless expense in foreign superfluities," Franklin observed with satisfaction, "some thought it had its share of influence in producing that growing plenty of money which was observable for several years after its publication." The popularity of *The Way to Wealth* has gathered momentum from that day to this. In 1928 Lewis J. Carey, in *Franklin's Economic Views*, remarked that it had been published "in most of the written languages of the world and has at the present time passed through about one thousand editions in the English and about three hundred in foreign languages." After devoting fifty-six pages to listing editions of *The Way to Wealth*, Paul Leicester Ford, the bibliographer of Franklin, finally gave up and announced that it was "simply impossible to find and note all the editions." The compilation of a reasonably complete bibliography of this single tract would be a lifework.

Whatever one may think of Franklin's philosophy, it has been the most influential social gospel in America to this day. Franklin was widely read in the colonial period. His wisdom was quoted with approval in newspapers and enjoyed the flattery of imitation. Since his own lifetime, his reputation has grown and his influence has magnified. Elsewhere I have discussed his influence on the Gilded Age.[2] Even yet, few other authors of books of wisdom have been so widely quoted in America. Newspapers have used his sayings for fillers. Business houses still issue Franklin calendars with his proverbs conspicuously printed. Trade publications in every business from the oil industry to the casket makers invoke the wit and wisdom of *The Way to Wealth*. The editors of daily newspapers can always find an apt quotation from Franklin as a springboard for an editorial. Franklin is still a live au-

[2] Louis B. Wright, "Franklin's Legacy to the Gilded Age," *Virginia Quarterly Review* 22 (1946):268–79.

thor and philosopher who conveys to millions of Americans the gospel of success first crystallized for us by our Elizabethan ancestors.

During the nineteenth century Franklin's proverbial wisdom was adapted in many publications designed to encourage youth to follow a regimen that would insure material success. Freeman Hunt, editor of *The Merchant's Magazine*, published in 1850 a volume entitled *Worth and Wealth: A Collection of Maxims, Morals, and Miscellanies for Merchants and Men of Business*, which borrowed from Franklin and other authors providing similar aphorisms. Hunt in his various writings emphasized that the honest pursuit of wealth was a Christian duty.

In the next generation, another compiler of bourgeois wisdom, T. L. Haines, borrowed Hunt's title and published in Chicago *Worth and Wealth, or the Art of Getting, Saving, and Using Money* (1883), which also pillaged Franklin for suitable proverbs. "Business is King," Haines announced, and proceeded to embroider that theme. "The saint of the nineteenth century," he declared, "is the good merchant; he is wisdom for the foolish, strength for the weak, warning to the wicked, and a blessing to all. Build him a shrine in bank and church, in the market and exchange, or build it not: no saint stands higher than the saint of trade."

In our own generation the saints of trade have had their halos too often tarnished for us to accept Haines's hyperbolic eulogy of the man of business. Nevertheless, deeply ingrained in American consciousness is the doctrine of self-reliance, of the desirability of conducting one's life with prudence sufficient to insure temporal success. Many Americans still take pride in being self-made men. The belief is still general that hard work and thrift are virtues to be prized. If sobriety is less honored with us than it was in Puritan Boston, at least we do not yet condone bacchanalian intemperance. Traditional middle-class virtues remain entrenched in great segments of American society.

Although we have reason to lament shoddy craftsmanship and a lack of pride in workmanship exhibited in some industries, this collapse is not yet the rule. Deep in American thinking is the conviction that hard work and attention to duty will bring rewards. Still widespread is the belief that good fortune and success are determined by man's own efforts. Ambition to rise in the world has not been demolished by the revolutionaries who would smash the Establishment. We are not about to join the communes. Traditions that date from the colonial period and before are here to stay—at least for the foreseeable future.

V

The British Tradition
in America in Retrospect

WITHIN THE MEMORIES of most of us, a tremendous change has occurred in the social composition and cultural development of the United States. To the older generation on both sides of the Atlantic, the United States will remain a sort of extension of the British world, another part of the English-speaking domain. We have all listened to countless speeches on the hands-across-the-sea theme, on our community of interests, and on the vitality of our common cultural heritage.

For a century and more the United States was the happy hunting ground of the itinerant British lecturer, who came over into Macedonia as a missionary to bring enlightenment to backward colonials. The populace of the United States has had a singular and almost pathetic zest for "improvement," and the man-hours consumed in listening to cultural "messages" from overseas are too astronomical for calculation. Not every listener, however, went away improved and sweetened. Many Americans have harbored a sour view of Great Britain that can be traced to the stupidity and the condescension of some lecturer from overseas. To the disgruntled listener he represented Great Britain just as a loud and blatant type from this side of the Atlantic too often signifies the genus Americanus.

On both sides of the Atlantic we long took for granted that the United States was a predominantly Anglo-Saxon country that had inherited its language, its legal tradition, its predominant religions, and most of its manners and customs from Great Britain. Of late, social historians have been taking a second look at the United States and questioning older presuppositions.

Although British America in the colonial period was also

a refuge for Germans, Frenchmen, and other Europeans, the majority of the settlers came from England, Scotland, Wales, and northern Ireland. With the exception of the Catholics who came to Maryland, most of these immigrants were Protestants with the peculiar but varied qualities of British Protestantism of this period. Even after the turn of the nineteenth century, English and Scottish immigration remained heavy, though by the 1830s we were beginning to acquire large increments of settlers from southern Ireland. In the thirty years between 1830 and 1860 nearly 2 million people, or approximately 71 percent of the total immigration from the United Kingdom, came from southern Ireland. But after 1860 the immigration from the rest of the United Kingdom again rose, and the Irish accounted for less than 50 percent of the immigration from the British Isles from 1860 to the present time.

Well over half of the total number of immigrants to the United States from all countries in the period from 1800 to 1870 were of British stock. But beginning in 1871 the proportion of British immigrants dropped sharply. The heaviest decade for immigration to the United States was the period from 1900 through 1910, when we received more than 8.5 million immigrants. Only a shade over 1.5 million of these were British.

During the First World War, old Americans became alarmed at the dilution of the British stock, and in 1917 we began to enact a series of immigration laws designed to restrict immigration in favor of the traditional stock. Lawmakers were careful of their language, but concern to perpetuate the traditional stock lay behind the immigration act of 1917 and subsequent laws. The act of 1921 established a quota system limited to 3 percent of the number of any nationality living in the United States. A revision of the law in 1924 restricted the quotas to 2 percent, based on the census of 1890, which favored British stock. The so-called National Origins Act of 1929 limited the total number of immigrants admitted in any one year to 150,000 and based the proportionate quotas on the "national origins" of the people of the

United States as of 1920, again favoring the British stock.

Within the past few years the proportion of Americans of British background has slipped below the 50-percent line, and now about 51 percent of the citizens of the United States are something other than Anglo-Saxon in origin. Whatever we are, more than half of us are not derived from British blood. In the eighteenth century Daniel Defoe wrote a poem called "The True Born Englishman" which ridiculed the pretensions of some of the 100-percent Englishmen of his day. He pointed out that the Englishman was a mongrel in whose veins flowed the blood of Picts, Scots, Danes, Saxons, Jutes, Normans, French, and heaven knows who else. The modern American is even more hopelessly confused in his blood strains. He may be a mixture of almost anything, and perhaps therein lies the secret of his vitality.

Accompanying the shift in the statistical basis of American blood strains we have had a more subtle change in our cultural attitudes. How far-reaching this change has been and what its effect will be, no one can say. But observers profess to see a marked differentiation from the culture of Great Britain. Clearly there is some change. Certainly few American intellectuals today feel any sense of filial piety toward Great Britain in the Henry James manner. Even fewer Americans care what Englishmen think ought to be the standard of English speech. In California I once heard a westerner refer to an English visitor as a "nice fellow in spite of his Oxford brogue," thus adding insult to injury with the Irish word *brogue*.

One of the most disturbing elements in the weakening of the British tradition is the falling off in the study of English history. Fewer and fewer courses in English history are being offered in American colleges and universities. English history is nonexistent in our high schools. A part of this flight from British history is the result of overcrowded curricula. But there is also an observable loss of interest in British history on the student level and on the part of faculty members.

The nature of the British tradition and its significance in

the development of our civilization are themes in which I have been interested for many years. If I repeat here things that I may have said elsewhere, I do it in the assurance that few have ever seen the words in print.

Before we sound the knell for British influence in American culture, we would do well to appraise its strength and try to see how profound modern changes may be. In my opinion, the cultural influence of the British tradition, as distinguished from any contemporary influence of the British nation, is almost as persistent as it was in the eighteenth and nineteenth centuries. But there are subtle differences in attitudes and emphasis.

Precisely how strong was the influence of British culture in America in the nineteenth century? It was strong enough to assimilate all other cultures in a fashion rarely seen before in history. We accept that assimilation as a matter of course and think nothing of it. Even some of our more rabid Anglophobes themselves illustrate the assimilation into the traditional cultural pattern. One of the curious ironies of history is the violence with which patriotic societies demand that 100-percent Americans conform to the culture of Britain. To be sure, the Daughters of the American Revolution may not be aware of what they are doing, but they are earnestly carrying on a propaganda to prevent any declaration of cultural independence from Britain. The truth is that we have inherited a great tradition that we have made our own, and we are often not aware of its British origins. I do not mean to suggest that American conditions have not modified and altered many aspects of Anglo-Saxon culture, but I do mean that we have taken over from the past a whole body of tradition that has made us the kind of people we are.

One of our inherited characteristics is cultural conservatism, which, from Jamestown in 1607 to the last western frontier at the end of the nineteenth century, has resulted in a compulsion to reproduce the best of the old civilization that the settlers had known. We have heard much in our time about the influence of the frontier on American life, a frontier that is reputed to have provided an opportunity to break the traditional shell of society, to stimulate originality, novelty, and freedom, to create a new kind of man and woman, etc. The facts are that settlers on the American frontier, from first to last, struggled to preserve and perpetuate the old, *not* to create something new. Few people have been more intent on reproducing the patterns of old society than the pioneers who settled the successive frontiers of our country.

In every community there was always a group who sometimes self-consciously called themselves the "better element." They were the ones who battled against lawlessness and nonconformity, who saw to it that religion, learning, and good manners were reestablished in the molds familiar in the society they had left.

In colonial America the settlers in each region sought in their several ways to reproduce the society of that portion of Britain which they represented. They were all determined not to let their children grow up barbarous in the wilderness. These Englishmen, Scots, and Welshmen were creating homes in a new world; they were not intending to return to Britain; they did not feel "displaced" and rootless. They were soon at home in the New World, because they had brought with them those intangible elements of the mind and spirit which kept them from feeling alien in a strange land. That process was to go on for three centuries, until all the land between the Atlantic and the Pacific had been brought under the sway of a people speaking the English language, living under English law, and conducting their lives under a system of manners, ethics, and morality developed in the British Isles.

In the agrarian South, notably in Virginia and Maryland, we developed a landed aristocracy that sought to imitate the county families of England. Land of course was the key to the development of this aristocracy. Most of the Tidewater aristocrats of the seventeenth and eighteenth centuries were descended from very plain folk indeed. They had come to America to improve their economic lot, to escape a burden of debts at home, to find opportunity to establish their families as landed and prosperous people.

54

A vast amount of effort and ink has been wasted by American genealogists trying to trace these families to someone of noble or genteel pretensions in England. In most cases they can't. The significant thing, however, is not what these people *were* before they arrived, but what they *wanted to become*, and what they *did become*. They brought with them an ideal of the Renaissance gentleman. Sometimes they brought along the very textbooks that English gentlemen had used as handbooks: Sir Thomas Hoby's translation of Castiglione's *Book of the Courtier*, Henry Peacham's *Compleat Gentleman*, or Richard Brathwaite's *English Gentleman* and *English Gentlewoman*.

They established themselves along the rivers of Virginia and Maryland as landed proprietors; they tried to bring up their sons in the classical tradition; and sometimes they sent them back to England for their education. They remembered one fundamental principle that characterized the English country gentleman: the notion that privilege carried with it responsibility. And, like their counterparts in Britain, the Tidewater gentry became the social backbone of the new country. They reestablished English law and justice; they early developed an enormous interest in constitutional theory and practice; and they acquired a skill and facility for government which made the transition in 1776 and 1787, from colonies to nation, relatively easy. The special qualities of Jefferson, Madison, Marshall, Washington, and many other American leaders may be attributed to the generations of traditional responsibility which lay behind them.

The religion of Virginia was the Church of England, adapted to local conditions. Robert Carter, for example, wrote his agent in London in 1720 to see that his three sons were sent to proper schools and given religious training. "As I am of the Church of England way, so I desire they should be," he wrote. "But the high-flown up top notions and the great stress that is laid upon ceremonies, any farther than decency and conformity, are what I cannot come into the reason of. Practical godliness is the substance—these are but the shell."

This passage is significant, for it implies another philosophic quality that Americans have inherited from the British, and that is the sense of the value of the practical, even in religion. We are pragmatists. "Will it work," the Englishman and the American always want to know. We are not interested in finespun logical theories. Or closely articulated philosophic systems. Or a fabric of theory, however beautiful in its details. We want a system that works, and we will sacrifice logic and theoretical order to achieve a workable program, whether it concerns our souls, our social welfare, or our political future.

Carter's attitude toward religion also illustrates the traditional English notion that orderly society requires respect for, and adherence to, the church as one of the pillars of the social order. That idea, to be sure, was no English monopoly, but it was consistently demonstrated by the British who settled in the New World, whether they were Catholics in Maryland, Anglicans in Virginia or Carolina, or Puritans in New England. And that notion our settlers carried with them across the continent.

When American historians and sociologists write about the impact of Puritanism on our society, they sometimes sound as if they believed Puritanism to be a New England invention, molded in Boston, for sale to such other parts of the country as would take it. Puritanism did find the climate of New England congenial, and there it flourished mightily, but it was an importation from Old England.

Few English qualities have been more pervasive than Puritanism, for Puritanism emphasized and magnified certain qualities of English character that have had an enormous influence in our own development. The ethical and moral inheritance that we received from England was not of course *exclusively* Puritan, but Puritan *interpretation* of ethical and moral problems has colored all of our later attitudes. The seventeenth-century English Puritans had a deep conviction that they were God's elect, the chosen people, destined to inherit this world and the next.

We verbalized a political philosophy in the 1840s which we called Manifest Destiny—our destiny to take all of the

North American continent that seemed good to us – but we did not invent Manifest Destiny. It was a legacy from seventeenth-century England.

We Americans, I am reliably informed, sometimes irritate our English brethren beyond endurance with our bumptiousness, our assertion that ours is God's country, that we enjoy the special favor of the Almighty, that, in short, we are the elect. That is an old story to the historian who surveys the common background of Great Britain and the United States. We Anglo-Saxons, with the authority of Puritan theology, have been telling everybody that for at least four hundred years.

Indeed, Englishmen of the seventeenth century were convinced that God spoke only English. It was true that in his omniscience, he could comprehend petitions from other folk, but his major concern was with the divinely-appointed English. It was an English parson, Lewis Hughes, who explained in 1621 that God in his wisdom had kept the Bermuda Islands hidden in a mist to prevent their discovery by the Spaniards until Englishmen were ready to take them over. In gratitude, said Hughes, for "the goodness of Almighty God in keeping these Islands secret . . . till now that it hath pleased his Holy Majesty to discover and bestow them upon his people of England," only pious immigrants should be allowed to settle in that paradise of the Western Sea.

We have maintained our inherited conviction of divine favor. I recall that during World War I, both English and American propagandists quoted as evidence of German arrogance and impiousness the motto found on German military equipment, "Gott Mit Uns." Everybody knew that God was with us English-speaking people.

Puritan beliefs help to account for the English and American genius for finding a moral justification for almost every action that seems desirable at the time. We have a deep compulsion to rationalize our social and political conduct on moral grounds, even when our actions are ethically dubious. During most of the eighteenth century, England and New England had almost a monopoly of the African slave trade, carried on with incredible cruelties. Yet pious shipping magnates of Bristol and Liverpool, Boston and Newport, were accustomed to fall on their knees in their churches and give thanks to God that they had been the instruments for bringing so many heathen souls to salvation—at so much a head. And when the traffic became unprofitable, Puritans set out to chastise the purchasers of those same heathen souls.

The Puritan conviction of righteousness has had a profound effect on our national character. It has given us strength; but it has also made us unloved by our neighbors.

During the controversy over slavery and the ensuing Civil War, both sides invoked the Bible and quoted Scripture to prove the moral rightness of their positions. Only a people steeped in the casuistry of English Protestantism of the seventeenth century could have proved so skillful in finding moral justification for both sides in that great debate.

In that period we saw a conflict between two notable qualities inherited from our British forebears. In the agrarian South, planters who tried to emulate the English country gentry were highly individualistic and made a fetish of privacy in the conduct of their own affairs. Meddling in your neighbor's business might cost you your life in a duel. In the Puritan North, village and town life had accustomed the populace to greater community concern over all that went on. Furthermore, the Puritan had cultivated the notion that he was his brother's keeper, and he became adept at plucking the mote out of his brother's eye. It was second nature for him to crusade for the Lord. Equipped with only a half-truth, clothed in a sense of his own virtue, he was eager to confute wickedness in others. The conflict between these two points of view, both essentially English, was inevitable. These two types we still have with us, and they still regard each other with profound distaste. Self-righteous meddlesomeness is one of our besetting, and congenital, sins.

The business civilization of the United States, its emphasis on commerce and trade, its acceptance of materialistic values, and its glorification of the cult of business success are frequently regarded today as American inventions of the late nineteenth and twentieth centuries. Nothing could be farther from the truth. These qualities are also a direct inheritance from sixteenth- and seventeenth-century England, transmitted to the New World by Puritans, Anglicans, and Quakers—all of whom equated diligence, thrift, sobriety, and industry with godliness. They frowned on most of the indulgences calculated to waste either money or time. Indeed, one of the Puritans' greatest concerns was to prevent the wasting of "God's precious time." Work for work's sake became a virtue.

Of all the religious groups that helped to civilize the successive frontier regions of the United States, none was more influential in transmitting traditional learning than the Scotch-Irish Presbyterians. They began to arrive in large numbers from Ulster early in the eighteenth century, and for the rest of the century they were an important factor in the American *Drang nach Westen.* From their numbers came the most invincible frontiersmen. They entered by the thousands through the port of Philadelphia, pushed beyond the peaceful Germans in the backcountry, and seized land from the Indians where it suited them.

The Scots brought with them an Old Testament type of religion. Their God was an avenging Jehovah, and they were convinced of their own calling to be the instruments for the carrying out of God's will. Seeing a parallel between themselves and the children of Israel, they looked upon the Indians as Canaanites, whose lands might be taken by the Chosen People. The Old Testament, moreover, supplied them with ample authority for exterminating the Indians, whom they identified as the Amalekites, for did not Jehovah enjoin his people to smite the heathen and destroy them root and branch?

The Ulster Scots also brought with them a bitter hatred of the English government, which had tried to force upon them conformity to the established church. When the controversies leading to the Revolution occurred, these dissident

Scots threw their weight against England in favor of independence. Had it not been for the Presbyterian Scots, the Revolution might have turned out differently.

Their great cultural contribution as frontiersmen was in transmitting respect for classical learning and in establishing schools and colleges in each successive frontier region until English-speaking people had reached the Pacific coast. The Scottish dominie believed that Latin and Greek were necessary to salvation. Princeton University is the most famous monument to the zeal of the Scotch-Irish Presbyterians, but there were many other academies, colleges, and universities which owed their founding to the Scots.

The Scotch Presbyterian ministers accompanied the frontiersmen into the wilderness and shared their lives and their hardships. They were often teachers as well as preachers. Many a fighting parson also organized the settlers and led them in the warfare against the Indians. Typical was John Elder, a minister in western Pennsylvania from 1738 to 1791. He served as a captain of militia and was accustomed to preach with a loaded musket across his pulpit. A graduate of the University of Edinburgh, he was a classical scholar, equally at home in tracing the wanderings of Ulysses or tracking down the most recent Indian marauder.

More famous even than Elder was Dr. John McMillan, an educator and minister in the backcountry of Pennsylvania, Tennessee, and Kentucky. Dr. McMillan was known for his learning, both classical and sacred. Traveling on one occasion with the Reverend Joseph Patterson to a meeting of the Pittsburgh presbytery, the two parsons stopped at a tavern for refreshment. The tavernkeeper set out two goblets of whiskey, the accepted beverage among the Scotch-Irish, lay or clerical. Before drinking, Mr. Patterson offered a prayer. After the custom of the time he prayed long and earnestly, reminding God of the accumulated events since the preachers had last passed that way. Dr. McMillan, weary and thirsty, quietly drank his own glass and then downed the other glass too. When Patterson finally said "Amen" and opened his eyes, he was distressed to find two empty glasses.

Remembering a scriptural injunction, Dr. McMillan reminded him, "My brother, the Bible teaches us both to watch and to pray."

These Presbyterians were practical, hardheaded folk. But they were the apostles of religion and learning. They insisted that every child know at least enough to read the Bible and the Shorter Catechism. They distributed tracts and books. And they often taught both children and adults. Invariably they insisted on an educated ministry, and they established seminaries in every frontier region to maintain the supply of learned preachers, and to provide higher education for the laity as well. Learning to them did not mean mere theological learning. It meant a solid grounding in the classics.

Higher education in America owes a tremendous debt to the Scotch Presbyterians, who believed that an education was worth almost any sacrifice. Like the English Puritans, they too had a stubborn conviction that they were divinely appointed to carry out a mission. "O Lord, grant that I may alway be right," one of them prayed, "for thou knowest that I am hard to turn."

The British tradition in education, especially the Scottish ideal of classical learning as represented by a large number of scholars from the University of Edinburgh, helped to give each region of our country the nucleus of a system of higher learning.

How was the British tradition transmitted and perpetuated? We have indicated the importance of religion in translating ethical and moral principles to the new country. We have also suggested some of the educational influences. These are themes for volumes, and we can only hint at them here.

But we are likely to overlook some of the most obvious and potent means of transmitting the tradition. We accept the English language and English literature as a matter of course and rarely stop to consider the implications of that heritage. It may be objected by some purists that we really do not speak the same language. But we might observe in passing that many forms and pronunciations that bookish

Englishmen today frown upon and sometimes, in their lofty commentary on American diction, call "Americanisms" are traditional usages common in England before Victorian grammarians introduced artificial and elegant "improvements." We need not worry too much about our linguistic differences. The motion picture, radio, and television will soon reduce it all to the common denominator of the networks.

The way the English language has assimilated every other language in the United States is a phenomenon rare in history. No country of the same size, and of similar complexity in national and linguistic stock, has ever accepted a common language so easily and so quickly as the United States. Nowhere has the melting pot operated more efficiently than in language. The non-English-speaking immigrant has shown a lamentable haste in giving up his native speech. No law forced him to learn English. None was needed. It was simply the thing to do, and he did it. Many an immigrant's children deliberately refused to learn their parent's native tongue, for anything except the common speech of America set them apart, and they all wanted to conform.

The question of whether a common language has been an asset in maintaining good relations between the United States and Great Britain has occasionally been raised. Some have argued that we understand each other too well, that diplomacy, like opera, is more successful when not too comprehensible. That, however, is not pertinent to my present discussion.

Second only to the influence of a common language as a unifying force in our culture has been the impact of English literature. We Americans simply inherited a great literature, took it over as our own, and until recently knew no other. We read English books—if we read any at all. When we went to school we studied English classics. Until this generation the most important single book in America was the King James Version of the Bible. Apart from its religious implications, it was a literary classic written in language of such simplicity and dignity that it made a universal appeal.

Its poetry, its sentence rhythms, and its diction influenced the speech and style of Englishmen and Americans for three centuries. Households that had no other book possessed a Bible and read it. It was no mere religious talisman. It was in itself a whole library which stimulated the imaginations of generations and gave them a feeling for words, for fine prose and poetry, for metaphor and color in language. The deserved place of the King James Version of the Bible in the affections of the American people is indicated by widespread objections to the American Revised Standard Version. One young woman of my acquaintance, whose sense of chronology was less developed than her judgment of literature, exclaimed, "The King James Version was good enough for St. Paul, and it's good enough for me."

Next to the Bible, the works of Shakespeare have enjoyed the greatest and longest popularity. It would be impossible to estimate the influence of Shakespeare as a literary carrier of the English tradition. He has had a triple role in our cultural development. First, the theater in every region found that Shakespeare always supplied a safe repertoire. Second, every American with any literary pretensions had Shakespeare in his library and read him. And third, for generations selections from Shakespeare occupied an important place in American schoolbooks and were considered excellent for speech and recitation purposes. Country editors were fond of beginning articles with an apt quotation from Shakespeare, and prairie politicians quoted him and the Bible as evidence of their fitness for office.

Shakespeare was deemed sufficiently moral and fit even for Puritan Boston, where *Othello*, for example, was presented as a "moral lecture" against jealousy. Delegations of Indian chiefs were sometimes entertained with performances of Shakespeare. *Richard III* appears to have edified them greatly. Indeed, *Richard III* was a favorite play on the American frontier. Traveling companies of players took Shakespeare to the Middle West long before the railroads reached those raw settlements, and Shakespeare was a staple of dramatic fare in California during the gold rush. Amateurs acted and recited Shakespeare. He was one of the means of Americanizing the sons and daughters of foreign immigrants, *foreign* being used in the usual American sense of "non-British." The son of a Polish immigrant might deliver Mark Antony's oration over dead Caesar, or the daughter of Italian parents might choose Portia's speech on mercy for a Friday afternoon recitation in her school.

What did Shakespeare do for successive generations of Americans? The answer is complex and cannot be answered in a paragraph. Certainly Shakespeare held up to millions of readers an appreciation of the nuances of language well used. It also gave them a sense of continuity in a cultural tradition. We have extracted moral lessons from Shakespeare as a bee takes honey from flowers. The Anglo-Saxon's capacity for finding ethical principles in literature is phenomenal. Generations of Americans have mined Shakespeare for useful and didactic quotations.

Other English authors were also influential in America. In the eighteenth century Addison and Steele were great teachers of the American public. Nearly every literate household had copies of the *Spectator*. We have Benjamin Franklin's description of how he deliberately imitated essays in the *Spectator*. From Addison and Steele Americans learned manners and acquired a certain amount of urbanity. A little later, Alexander Pope was popular, especially his *Essay on Man*, which was widely read and often quoted for its apt moral sayings. In frontier days in Kentucky the *Essay on Man* was reprinted in newspaper offices. During the first half of the nineteenth century the most popular authors in the West were Sir Walter Scott and Lord Byron. Steamboats on the Mississippi and Ohio rivers were named for characters in Scott or Byron, and their works were eagerly sought after. As fast as transportation could provide copies, the books were distributed throughout the frontier West.

The popularity of British authors may have been flattering, but it was not profitable to the writers: until 1891 there was no copyright protection for British books, and we shamelessly pirated British publications. American writers like James Fenimore Cooper complained that publishers preferred to bring out British authors because they did not have to pay royalties to writers from overseas. But that is only part of the story. Our public traditionally looked to Britain for literature, and they even liked best those American writers who wrote as nearly as possible like British authors.

For nearly three centuries schoolbooks provided another powerful means of transmitting the British literary tradition to America. After the Revolution a group of New England textbook authors, the best known being Noah Webster, set about deliberately to prepare texts purged of English propaganda. Webster went so far as to change spellings and pronunciations. His famous "blue-back speller" left the *u* out of such words as *labour* and simplified the spelling of words like *plough*—all for patriotic reasons. He also attempted to establish the dialect of rural Connecticut as standard American pronunciation. That, however, was too much for Virginians and others who continued to prefer English spelling books and readers—one in particular, John Walker's *A Critical Pronouncing Dictionary and Expositor of the English Language* (London, 1791)—which gave them authority for such pronunciations as "gyarden."

Webster and his fellow New Englanders made a brave struggle to root out Anglicisms, but, popular as their books were, they did not altogether succeed. In time the country reacted against the New England school of textbookmakers, whose brand of patriotism was too provincial—and too Federalistic—for the rest of the country.

The most complete rebellion came in the West with the publication of a series of famous readers compiled by William Holmes McGuffey, a Scotch Presbyterian preacher who had been brought up on the Ohio frontier. From the appearance of McGuffey's *First* and *Second Reader* in Cincinnati, in 1836, to 1900, more than 122,000,000 copies were sold. When we remember that each copy was used over and over until it was literally worn to shreds, we can get some notion of the millions of children who received most of their elementary education out of these books.

Although McGuffey did sprinkle through his textbooks a quantity of patriotic speeches from American orators and a few immortal and erroneous anecdotes, like Parson Weems's story of George Washington and the cherry tree, the major portion of the selections printed in his books came from standard British writers from Shakespeare to Macaulay. Lest the pupil miss the application of some of the passages, McGuffey made the moral explicit. For instance, a dialogue between Cassio and Iago from *Othello* is entitled "Folly of Intoxication." Perhaps McGuffey's inclusion of Mrs. Felicia Hemans's romantic poem "The Landing of the Pilgrim Fathers" did more to establish the settlers at Plymouth in American imaginations than all the labors of William Brewster and Miles Standish. But do not forget that Mrs. Hemans was English.

McGuffey's philosophy of materialistic optimism is authentic middle-class doctrine of the English seventeenth century transferred to the American frontier, and his plenitude of selections from English authors simply confirms this gospel, so congenial to the promotional spirit of America. McGuffey never let his pupils forget the social significance of literature. He was careful to include in the *Fifth Reader* a selection from Blackstone's *Commentaries* on the "Origin of Property." For all McGuffey's nationalistic fervor, he represents an almost pure strain of British culture modified only by its transplantation to the West.

The fact that McGuffey thought it well to include a passage from Blackstone's *Commentaries* in his *Fifth Reader* is significant of the prestige of that work in America. Blackstone actually had a far greater influence in America than in England, and long after his *Commentaries* were obsolete at home, the work remained the bible of American lawyers, who got most of their education in jurisprudence from it. Few books have had a more profound effect on the legal traditions of a people. It is estimated that more than 1,000 copies of Blackstone were shipped to the colonies before the first American edition of 1771–72. In the following century more copies of Blackstone were bought in America than were sold in Great Britain.

Every schoolchild, of course, has heard that we received our basic law from England, our notions of individual liberty, trial by jury, habeas corpus, and all the other guarantees of freedom. But few stop to inquire how the common law and the traditions of liberty implied under it have been perpetuated. In the early days, of course, we simply took over English law and English legal handbooks, reports, and commentaries, and our lawyers conducted procedures as best they knew in accordance with English practice. After the Revolution we made such superficial changes as were necessary but retained the English legal tradition. Occasionally patriots were disturbed at this dependence. In 1811, for example, on the eve of our second war with Great Britain, the legislature of Kentucky passed a law forbidding attorneys to cite precedents from English courts later than July 4, 1776. Until our own century, Blackstone's *Commentaries* continued to be the most significant single vehicle for conveying to Americans traditional legal thought and opinion.

For more than three centuries the strongest elements in our civilization have come from an inheritance that goes back to that vital period in history which, for want of a better word, we call the English Renaissance. The age of Shakespeare comes near the center of that germinal period. At the beginning we see the vigor and strength of the Tudor monarchs who laid the foundations for England's development as a world power. Toward the end of the period we see the debates, conflicts, and political growth consequential to the struggle between the Stuart monarchs and the stubborn English people, a period of controversy that ended with the Glorious Revolution of 1688 and the irrevocable (we hope) establishment of certain fundamental concepts of the freedom of the individual within a frame of law.

The civilization developed within the British Isles between 1485 and 1715, the period of the Tudors and Stuarts, had such extraordinary vigor that it has not yet lost its dynamic power. It carried over to the New World and became the assimilative force that created the American people as we are. Again I want to repeat that we are not mere replicas of Englishmen, Scots, Welshmen, or Irishmen, for we have been an eclectic folk and have taken much from other people. But in general our fundamental qualities derive from British civilization.

The question being asked now is whether the cultural tradition that Americans inherited, and that exerted such a profound influence in the past, retains its dynamic strength. What is the impact of the old tradition on the modern world? Does it still have the capacity to assimilate and to create afresh a relatively homogeneous culture derived from the past but not subservient to it?

Without doubt the British cultural tradition is still a force of genuine significance in American life. The stresses of our time have revealed the basic strength that we have inherited from the past. We have spent a great deal of energy and printer's ink surveying the nature of our legacy from all of Western civilization and its contributions to our spiritual, intellectual, political, and economic welfare. We have been at pains to study with particular care that portion of our inheritance that came from Great Britain, and we have a healthy regard for its continuing value.

But we would be inaccurate in our observations if we failed to take note of changes of far-reaching significance for both countries. Unfortunately, few Englishmen have sufficient knowledge of the United States to appraise the changes correctly, and most Americans, bereft of historical perspective, are unaware of any break with the past. Yet there is a break with the tradition that I have tried to describe. That explains why the visiting British lecturer, who frequently comes to the United States with a stock of ideas that show little advance over Dickens's *American Notes*, is often a spectacular anachronism. For some centuries Americans were inclined to believe that British intellectual goods were best. For example, British books, as I have tried to show, shaped our thinking. But there is serious doubt whether that condition any longer prevails. "Who reads a British book?" some millions of Americans could ask without getting an affirmative answer. A cynic might retort that the question really ought to be, "Who reads a book?" The facts are that contemporary British literature is not an important export to the United States, as it was in the mid-nineteenth century, nor is the indigenous literature of the United States in our time very much affected by influences from the British side of the Atlantic. For reasons that are complex and partly conditioned by economic forces, we are going our separate literary ways, and neither country shows much awareness of what is happening outside of its own borders.

In an earlier time Americans looked to Great Britain for educational guidance and wisdom. But in our time that is no longer true. Though many of us lament what has happened to our schools, few Americans would think, as they might have thought even a few years ago, that the answer to our educational problem might be supplied through imitation of English methods. Even in our colleges and universities, despite the number of academic administrators who have profited from the benefaction of Cecil Rhodes, there is today no significant body of opinion that holds that English university life, even if it could be transplanted, would be either useful or desirable for us. That does not mean that we are complacent about what we have. Far from it. But it does mean that we no longer look back to the tradition that once seemed so important.

Perhaps the cultural changes that have taken place in the United States during the past half-century indicate the attainment of a maturity we previously lacked. With maturity has come a shift in the emphasis on traditional values. And on both sides of the Atlantic we would do well to forget much sentimental nonsense and to understand what this shift in emphasis means to both of us. It means that English ways and English ideas are less easily understood and accepted on our side of the Atlantic. For better or for worse we are more inclined to go our own way in cultural matters. In some quarters there is an almost jaunty disdain of the old and a skepticism about its current validity for us. Students from Great Britain will find America more complex and more difficult to understand than it was in the nineteenth century. Unhappily, too many who set themselves up as expositors of contemporary American civilization are still conditioned by clichés perpetuated by Dickens and Kipling. For our part, some of our younger scholars and interpreters are too inclined to disregard traditional influences of long standing, and to overemphasize the impact of non-British influences on the development of our civilization.

Since we are likely to be partners in a common cause for many years to come, Britain might profitably give serious attention to a fresh approach to the study of American civilization and of its own contributions to both our good and our bad qualities. And as for us, we shall do well to remember our immense debt to the Old World before we become too cocky, or allow any neochauvinism to disturb our ties with countries from which we still have much to learn.

VI

Shakespeare for Everyman:
Traditional Views

A FEW YEARS AGO I wrote a little book called *Shakespeare for Everyman*, which attempted to emphasize an obvious truth: that William Shakespeare did not write for college professors, professional critics, or even drama directors, but for the common run of mankind. I also tried to show that he had a superb sense of the theater, a perception of what would cause an audience to react favorably, even to the use of gags and slapstick that would tickle the groundlings in the yard as well as the gentry in the galleries.

Of course not every play that he wrote was a roaring success on first performance, for that would be too much to expect, but a surprising number scored immediately and have been good theater ever since. The test of Shakespeare's greatness has been the survival of his plays through centuries of adapters, "improvers," critics, schoolteachers, and theatrical innovators. It is true that a Shakespearean play as presented in the theater is sometimes hardly recognizable as the dramatist's original creation, but somehow no amount of maltreatment in any age has destroyed this dramatist, and he comes back restored to his pristine strength.

After the "improvers" of the Restoration and the first half of the eighteenth century, David Garrick came along to make a plea for the restoration of the true text of the poet. Garrick, it must be conceded, himself had tinkered with Shakespeare, but he repented, and if he did not appear at Drury Lane exactly in sackcloth and ashes, he did actively protest the worst of the adaptations. No longer in favor was Nahum Tate's 1681 version of *King Lear*, that inspired piece of idiocy that wrote into the text a love story between Edgar and Cordelia and ended with their marriage and old Lear

71

retiring to a place of meditation to ponder the whims of Fate.

Garrick, a theatrical producer of unusual acumen, realized that though Shakespeare wrote a century and a half before Garrick took over the management of Drury Lane, he needed little adaptation to make his work relevant to the eighteenth century (or to any age). Moreover, as a first-class theatrical craftsman, the dramatist had inserted most of the "business" needed to make his plays good entertainment in 1747 (or at any other time). A modern critic has complained that Shakespeare, unlike Shaw, did not write elaborate stage directions and that we do not know how he intended his plays to be acted. This critic obviously has not read the plays carefully. The text nearly always makes the author's intentions explicit.

Among the Shakespeare productions on this continent, those performed at the Oregon Shakespearean Festival at Ashland stand out for their excellence. Perhaps Ashland's greatest contribution to Shakespearean interpretation over the years has been its respect for the original text, the presentation of Shakespeare without distortion of meaning, without resort to irrelevant and disturbing gimmicks, and without doing obeisance to current fashion, however idiotic. The last is important, for no area of our culture has displayed more evidence of lunacy (unless it be politics) than the fluctuating fashions of the entertainment world.

A few years ago I saw in Ashland's open-air theater a presentation of *Pericles*, which I had always thought one of Shakespeare's least actable plays. A "fashionable" director would have performed it with every gimmick he could have dreamed up to give it contemporary "appeal." But Ashland performed it as Shakespeare wrote it—and made it an evening of genuine enjoyment. A rancher who had never darkened the door of a class in Shakespeare would have found it entertaining, as many undoubtedly did. This respect for Shakespeare's text has led me to say publicly and in print that Ashland has produced the best Shakespeare on this continent.

But lest I be misunderstood, let me hasten to make clear

that I am not maintaining that a drama director must not show originality, or that an actor must not deviate from some static interpretation of a character inherited from the past. Fresh interpretation is expected in any age. New ways of presenting the plays will occur to ingenious directors. But what I am trying to say is that distortion of the text to impose some current ideology, or some absurd gimmickry that distracts attention from the meaning of the play, does a disservice to the audience and demeans Shakespeare to mediocrity. Of examples of this disservice we have abundant evidence, and I shall have more to say about that in a moment.

No one can complain when an author or director uses Shakespeare as a point of departure for something else. *Kiss Me Kate* was a rollicking musical that gave pleasure to a multitude of theater-goers. But *Kiss Me Kate* did not pretend to be *The Taming of the Shrew*. It was avowedly something else, legitimate, entertaining, and a credit to the producers. But producers who palm off a mangled and distorted adaptation of any play of Shakespeare, and call it veritable Shakespeare, are taking money at the box office under false pretense. Shooting them at sunrise has been ruled out by the Supreme Court, but we might sentence them to listen to their own productions for a period of years. That would be cruel and unusual punishment, to be sure, but they would hardly be in a position to assert it.

We live in an age of violence and disorder, we are told, and to make Shakespeare "relate" to our times it is necessary to interpret his plays with violence, disorder, incoherence, and all the symptoms of our current ills. That view is wrong on several counts. First, it is unhistorical. Though our world seems to us disjointed, disturbed, and oppressive, actually, if we analyze earlier periods of history, they were far more disorderly, shackled, warlike, and dangerous than the present. Never has the world seen greater freedom and permissiveness—to the point of license—than at this moment. Shakespeare's own age was one of uncertainty, lack of freedom for the individual, war, violence, and fear of death from both plague and the hand of man. But that did not keep him from writing serene comedies like *A Midsummer Night's Dream*, boisterous farces like *The Taming of the Shrew*, or cosmic tragedies like *Hamlet* and *King Lear*. These tragedies, indeed, were filled with violence, but there was something else there that raised them far beyond the transient appeal of blood-and-thunder plays like Thomas Kyd's *The Spanish Tragedy*. The quality that saved Shakespeare's tragedies, in addition to immortal poetry, was the treatment of universal themes that are perennial in every age and country, themes that are not dependent on topicality for their relevance.

Any critical observer must be appalled at certain recent and current stage interpretations of Shakespeare because of their superficiality, their unhistorical approach, their wrong-headed ignorance of what the author was trying to say, and their deadly seriousness. We can forgive a director almost anything if he will not bore us to death with an inexorable, purposeful, punishing seriousness, as if William Shakespeare had been sent to flog us into recognition of the ills of the commonwealth or the wickedness of man.

Shakespeare was a great entertainer—among many other things—and not an avenging angel. But, a producer can airily assert, it does not matter what Shakespeare intended; it is what we can read into him that is important. Such a reason deserves the answer Lewis Theobald gave Alexander Pope when Pope inserted erroneous emendations in his edition of Shakespeare's works: "Very pretty, Mr. Pope, but don't call it Shakespeare."

Perhaps the most fashionable director of the moment is Peter Brook of the Royal Shakespeare Theatre, and his most talked about interpretation is the production of *A Midsummer Night's Dream* in which he makes the fairy scenes a study in sexual bestiality. In an essay on directorial tendencies entitled "Free Shakespeare" in *Shakespeare Survey*, no. 24 (1971), John Russel Brown of Birmingham University treads gingerly but finds fault with his neighbor's interpretation. Brook had asserted, with four-letter directness, that Oberon intended "to degrade Titania as a woman" by having her loved by Bottom the ass, "the crudest sex machine he can find." Brown objects that "the director has here left the text far behind," for Oberon does not choose a "sex machine" of any sort to degrade Titania, but expects her only to be plagued with hateful fantasies and "to love and languish" for any "vile thing." Furthermore, Bottom is not a beast but a man—like some others, momentarily with an ass's head—and hence, even if he intended to make love to Titania—which he does not—it would not be a case of bestiality as implied in Brook's perverse interpretation. But why belabor such arrant nonsense simply because it is momentarily fashionable?

Although it must have caused Brown some soul-searching to be critical of Brook in nearby Stratford, especially since Brook has been canonized as a dramatic messiah and widely imitated by lesser lights, Brown nevertheless concludes: "Most critics have proclaimed a new way of staging Shakespeare after seeing Brook's production, but what seems newest in his work is the theatrical playing with the text in order to invent business and discover an interpretation that suits his own interests and the actors with whom he is working." Very pretty, Mr. Brook (or is it?), but don't call it Shakespeare.

Brown ends his essay on a somewhat pessimistic note, for he really is implying that something ought to be done to "free Shakespeare" from any single-minded interpretation by a director, interpretation that distorts the meaning out of all countenance. So fashionable is this approach today, thanks in part to the influence of the Royal Shakespeare Theatre's recent innovations, that any deviation from the fashion is dangerous; but Brown suggests the desirability of finding "a director who would maintain close contact with the text and seek to avoid limiting the actors' work by a single-minded interpretation. He would be courting failure, but also attempting to release Shakespeare from confinement."

Another British critic, Gareth Lloyd Evans, has questioned the validity of the Royal Shakespeare Theatre's interpretations and expressed concern about the baleful influence of some of these interpretations on the understanding and enjoyment of Shakespeare. In "Shakespeare, the Twentieth Century, and 'Behaviourism'" (*Shakespeare Survey*, no. 20 [1967]), he analyzes some of the motivations of the company under the direction of Peter Hall. Hall believes, according to Evans, that producers must "try to express Shakespeare's intentions in terms that modern audiences can understand," for Hall has, says Evans, "a deep socio-philosophical purpose." It has been Hall's effort to " 'democratize' the social strata of the plays." Now it is one thing to present the plays in a way that the twentieth century can understand, but quite another to set one's self up as a social philosopher able to make Shakespeare a democrat in twentieth-century terms so that other democrats presumably will understand and enjoy him. Peter Hall's purpose and interpretation would have puzzled William Shakespeare to the point where he would have fled to the Mermaid Tavern for a few more drinks.

Evans continues his criticism by pointing out that, despite its frequent brilliance and cleverness, the Royal Shakespeare Theatre's emphasis on what he calls behaviorism "is often starkly apparent in comic scenes of a strong visual intensity that almost always has an immediate theatrical effect but often seems to be external to the text." A later essay by Evans entitled "The Reason Why: The Royal Shakespeare Season, 1968, Reviewed," in *Shakespeare Survey*, no. 22 (1969), emphasizes the deterioration of the poetic sense when interpretations depend on scenic effects rather than language. He concludes that in the new dispensation, the actors have no grasp of the power of Shakespeare's language but merely vulgarize the rendition of his poetry. Evans also reveals the self-defeating result of theatrical sensationalism. "Stratford made its most explicit committal to the era of permissiveness when it announced that Helen in [Marlowe's] *Dr. Faustus* was to appear naked. . . . She did indeed appear naked— and that is all. It is a respectable and traditional view that a sweet disorder in dress kindles wantonness, and the total exposure has an anaesthetic effect. Helen's appearance proved this." Reverting to Shakespeare, Evans comments, "Shakespeare seems to be moving inexorably into the background, to be replaced by image-making, which at its best is merely vivid and at its worst separated by the reality of the plays."

In his essay on Stratford's trend toward behaviorism, Evans ponders the influence of so highly respected a theatrical organization. He concludes that "the Royal Shakespeare Theatre may set a standard which could map the course of Shakespeare production for decades to come. In hands less skilful than those of the Royal Shakespeare Theatre the adaptation, and the resultant behaviorism which is its main flaw, would become unbearable. The long process of rediscovering Shakespeare and, through Shakespeare, the values of the past, undertaken by previous centuries, would have to begin again."

Some of Evans's worst fears have been realized, for recent dramatic directors, having drunk at Stratford's less than Pierian spring, return home to imitate what they think they have seen. The result is often a banality that drives audiences away in droves. But the real disaster is utter distraction from attention to the play itself as one ponders such marvels as an Elizabethan stage smothered in aluminum foil, courtesy of Reynolds Wrap, for a performance of *Twelfth Night*, or *Romeo and Juliet* set in a nineteenth-century circus with the lovers clambering into a van onstage. (Both of these miracles, I regret to say, recently astonished audiences at the Folger Shakespeare Library.)

The trend toward making Shakespeare "relate" to the present (and may God forgive me for using such clichés as *relate* and *relevant*) reached its ultimate absurdity in London, with Charles Marowitz's *Othello*—as one critic put it, "a rejigged *Othello*." It was indeed a total overhaul, a rewritten documentary on the race problem. Michael Billington, drama critic, recently commented in the *Manchester Guardian:* "Mr. Marowitz's boldest innovatory stroke is to make Othello and Iago represent contrasting black stereotypes: what Malcolm X called the House Negro, who totally accepts his master's system of values, and the Field Negro, who is a congenital revolutionary. Theatrically this yields any number of effective moments such as Iago's running scatalogical commentary on Othello's Uncle Tomist speech to the Venetian Senate or the Moor's belated refusal to fulfill a white audience's expectation by committing suicide." Not very pretty, Mr. Marowitz, and don't call it Shakespeare.

Although we live in an age that relishes absurdity, let us not get carried away completely. Marowitz's rewriting of *Othello* makes Nahum Tate's doctoring of *King Lear* look downright enlightened.

To go on enumerating perverse interpretations of Shakespeare in our time would be unsporting, like shooting ducks on a baited pond. Nevertheless, perhaps you would like to be reminded that "gay" theatrical interpreters of *As You Like It* have presented Rosalind and Celia as lesbian lovers. And *King Lear* is widely interpreted by Freudians as a play on the incestuous love of Cordelia and the old king. It is not enough to reveal the robust sex that Shakespeare treated with a sense of appropriateness to the situation; we must now probe in dark corners for perverted sex in order to be "with it."

We are so used to freakish novelties in the theater that no eccentric staging of Shakespeare any longer startles us: *Hamlet* with all the actors dressed in white; *King Lear* done up as a parcel of Eskimos; *Macbeth* acted by ancient proletarians with Lady Macbeth coming onstage carrying a churn; the Forest of Arden in *As You Like It* thickly populated with leather-jacketed Hell's Angels just off their motorcycles; and so on, ad infinitum. All of this we can take in stride — provided the director respects the text of the play and insists on his actors' reading their lines intelligently and intelligibly.

What is most grievous to a playgoer today is the high seriousness of so much theatrical eccentricity, with producers turned social reformers or forgetting that Shakespeare wrote to entertain. Although the genius of Shakespeare gave his plays a depth of meaning beyond the amusement of the moment, he never turned preacher. Furthermore, he never let his eyes stray far from the box office. Few writers or producers have ever been so careful to ascertain what an audience would pay to see, and few have tried so hard to please. This mundane concern paid off. Shakespeare's company prospered; he made enough money to buy the finest house in Stratford; and he could afford to retire early and live the life of a small town magnate. That is a good deal more than some of the fashionable purveyors of Shakespearean drama can say today. It would be unkind to reveal the vast deficits that some of the new interpreters have accumulated. Had not taxpayers' or foundation money bailed them out, they would have sunk without a trace before now.

If a company is induced by fashion to delete the merriment from Shakespeare or to substitute black humor of recent invention, it cannot complain when audiences seek entertainment elsewhere. High solemnity is an austere taste that ordinary mortals find hard to cultivate, especially high solemnity with a social purpose. Proof of man's bestiality, seen through Oberon's eyes, is not to the liking of most of us. Shakespeare's delight in a merry joke is surer to please. Most of us go to the theater for entertainment, not for reform or instruction. We may not always expect to laugh uproariously, and, in witnessing *King Lear* or *Hamlet*, we may experience a certain purgation through pity and fear, but that is incidental. We do not go primarily for the good of our souls. Shakespeare knew that better than most of his latter-day interpreters. That may explain why those theatrical producers who have presented Shakespeare without altering his meaning have achieved greater success—in reputation and at the box office—than the dramatic tinkers.

Blame for misrepresenting Shakespeare today must be widely shared. The producers are not alone responsible. The temper of the times accounts in part for it. Not long ago a film entitled *A Clockwork Orange* was widely acclaimed by critics for its trend-setting innovations. Any age that finds a movie like *A Clockwork Orange* an artistic treasure has something to answer for. An anonymous critic in the *Washington Star* observed of this manifestation: "There is a name for what *A Clockwork Orange* represents and it is depravity. Having seen it you walk quickly from the theater, looking neither to the right nor to the left, ashamed to be human, and in the night air there is a leathery rustling as of the wings of great bats."

The rustling of bats' wings, I am afraid, follows the misinterpretation of some of Shakespeare's plays. And audiences who are no lovers of bats are not going to risk the night air for the next showing.

Academic critics must also share responsibility for misrepresentations that invite disaster in the theater, for wide is the literary gate and broad is the way that leadeth to destruction. Producers like to feel that they keep up with scholarship and are aware of the mental workings of the cognoscenti. One trouble is that the cognoscenti themselves are vastly confused and, like lost sheep, follow some bellwether into the critical wilderness.

In 1964 a critic burst out of Poland like a bright new star, a certain Jan Kott, whose work was translated as *Shakespeare Our Contemporary* and at once became Holy Writ for all those who wanted to believe that Shakespeare had notions as perverse as ours. In the words of Prof. Alfred Harbage's British Academy lecture, "Shakespeare without Words" (1969), Kott reduces the plays of Shakespeare to unplayful "pantomime with reveries—in this case the critic's own." And he adds: "What emerges is a series of history plays in which automaton kings are cranked into lethal action by a senselessly cruel machine. *Macbeth* is one of those history plays, with no distinction perceptible between the occasion of the Thane's killing others and the occasion of his being killed. *King Lear* is a grotesque charade, presenting no tragic hero but a clutch of writhing clowns. *A Midsummer Night's Dream* is an exploration of lechery, in particular bestiality. *The Tempest* is a sigh of despair. You will have identified the book as Jan Kott's *Shakespeare Our Contemporary*. The method of the book is to ignore Shakespeare's words except for those taken out of context." You may, if you take the trouble to read Kott, see where Brook got his inspiration—if that is the word—for his interpretation of *A*

Midsummer Night's Dream, and where other producers have gone for a vision of the new truth.

Curiously, Kott's book, received with prayerful reverence by many Shakespeareans from Poland to Japan, was regarded, in Harbage's words, as so much ratsbane by the Russians. Incidentally, Russia has taken Shakespeare to its bosom. For a while they tried to make him speak in orthodox Marxist terms, but they soon gave that up. Now Shakespeare is played straight in scores of cities of Russia. In Leningrad I even saw a remarkable ballet based on *Hamlet* that had no political overtones. And it took a Russian critic, Grigori Kozintsev, to write a better book than Kott's, which was translated as *Shakespeare: Time and Conscience* (1966), but which had a Russian title that sounded like Kott's, *Our Contemporary: Shakespeare*. In Harbage's words, Kozintsev "reinvoked the more familiar Shakespeare, bright apostle of moral decency and the dignity of Man." Harbage wonders in his essay if Russia, called by another Russian scholar, R. M. Samarin, the "second home" of Shakespeare, "will become the only home, indeed the refuge of the pre-Kottian Shakespeare?"

Harbage concludes his own essay with the implied hope —if I read him correctly—that we can have a Shakespeare that is not doctrinal, not solemnly didactic, but a Shakespeare in which the play can weave its own spell without external distraction.

And let me add my own hope that we can again learn to laugh, to enjoy the humor that Shakespeare provided in his plays in such abundance. Of late, grimness has become a fashion, as if the world had not always seen suffering and misery and we had to mourn over it as something newly discovered. In the past the world learned to laugh so that it might endure; we have become afraid to laugh.

Shakespeare knew better. He had a remarkable sense of humor and a healthy zest for life. His humor is frequently earthy, sometimes coarse, but never smirking. His greatest comic character was Falstaff, "honest Jack Falstaff," whom

Shakespeare pictured with all his faults and all his reality, down to the last spatter of beer on his greasy doublet. For a brief moment I would like to commend this fat rogue to you as perhaps an antidote to some of the gloom that critics would leave with you.

Falstaff in our time may need some defense, for it is hard to derive any Freudian or sociological lessons worthy of study from this roistering old reprobate. Indeed, a friend of mine reports that he was invited to a class in Shakespeare in which the instructor was teaching *1 Henry IV*. This instructor spent a good part of the class hour apologizing for Shakespeare's necessity in creating Falstaff, "an irrelevancy and a blot on the play," inserted merely to please unsophisticated groundlings who demanded coarse entertainment. Another teacher of Shakespeare has endeavored to make the fat knight the subject of learned interpretation by treating the theme of "Falstaff as Symbol and Myth." Let me assure you that Falstaff in Shakespeare's mind was neither symbol nor myth but a very human vehicle for the expression of earthy humor.

It is true that Shakespeare was writing for a popular stage, and he inserted in his plays something for everybody. I once sat in the topmost gallery of the Old Vic Theatre in London, surrounded by charwomen, cabdrivers, and other working folk who had come to a play to be entertained, not edified. The play that night was *Love's Labor's Lost*. At intervals in the action the old cabbie sitting by me would give me a nudge and say, "That's a good 'un," as he laughed uproariously over the slapstick and clownery. Much of the word-play went over his head, to be sure, but Shakespeare did not neglect to include something for the cabbie, to provide humor on all levels. He realized that humor had a fundamental place in drama, as in life, and even in his most philosophical tragedies he added scenes that brought laughter to his audiences. No one who reads or sees *Hamlet* can fail to react to the comic pomposity of old Polonius or the humorous commentary of the gravediggers.

But let us return to Falstaff, Shakespeare's supreme comic

creation. If Falstaff pleased the groundlings, he also appealed to others. A seventeenth-century legend reports that Queen Elizabeth I was so taken with Falstaff that she demanded that Shakespeare show him in love, with the result that the dramatist wrote *The Merry Wives of Windsor*. For nearly 400 years readers and audiences have been laughing at this character, who has inspired not only actors but artists. Few of Shakespeare's characters have been the subject of more paintings and caricatures than Falstaff.

This is no place to attempt an analysis of the reasons for the popularity. Humor often defies analysis, and we need not murder to dissect this subject. Let us content ourselves with observing a few manifestations of Shakespeare's interpretation of this mountainous fat man, who was "not only witty . . . but the cause that wit is in other men" (2 *Henry IV*, I.ii. 9–10).[1] We laugh at him, and with him, not merely because of the incongruities of situation but because the play of Falstaff's wit constantly amuses us. In his verbal encounters with Prince Hal, we laugh at his adroit maneuvers as he parries the thrusts of his hilarious tormentor. We also laugh because Falstaff can laugh at himself. In our world full of solemn self-importance, the man who does not take himself too seriously wins our sympathy.

None of us ever knew a character precisely like Falstaff, but we have encountered people with some of his qualities. He is a rascal, to be sure, but as Sir Edmund Chambers comments in *Shakespeare: A Survey* (p. 125), the stuff of comedy is found in the fact that "Falstaff's intellectual faculties have survived the shipwreck" of his morality. "His quick wits are always ready to save him from some dire humiliation, to the brink of which he has been led by his cowardice or his greed. His mental resource is inexhaustible. No man is his master at a verbal retort, or in the gentle art of making the worse appear the better cause." He is ready with plausible reason to excuse his shortcomings. "Company, villainous company, hath been the spoil of me," he complains,

---

[1] Shakespeare quotes are from Louis B. Wright, *Folger Library General Reader's Shakespeare* (New York, 1960).

after observing that "I have not forgotten what the inside of a church is made of" (*1 Henry IV*, III.iii. 7–11). He will admit to evildoing but will not take the blame for it. "Thou hast done much harm upon me, Hal," he tells the prince. "God forgive thee for it! Before I knew thee, Hal, I knew nothing; and now am I, if a man should speak truly, little better than one of the wicked" (I.ii. 93–97).

The very monstrosity of Falstaff's impudence entertains us. When Prince Hal encounters him on the battlefield of Shrewsbury, Falstaff pretends to have killed Hotspur, but the prince exclaims, "Why, Percy I killed myself." Falstaff then coolly comments, "Didst thou? Lord, Lord, how this world is given to lying" (V.iv. 152–55).

Few passages are more memorable than Falstaff's apostrophe to honor as he contemplates the unpleasant possibility of death on the battlefield. Prince Hal has just scared him out of his wits by observing, "Thou owest God a death." Falstaff responds: " 'Tis not due yet; I would be loath to pay him before his day. What need I be so forward with him that calls not on me? Well, 'tis no matter; honor pricks me on. Yea, but how if honor prick me off when I come on? How then? Can honor set to a leg? No. Or an arm? No. . . . What is honor? A word. What is in that word honor? What is that honor? Air—a trim reckoning! Who hath it? He that died a Wednesday. Doth he feel it? No. Doth he hear it? No. 'Tis insensible then? Yea, to the dead. But will it not live with the living? No. Why? Detraction will not suffer it. Therefore I'll none of it. Honor is a mere scutcheon—and so ends my catechism" (V.i. 128–43).

Shakespeare in this passage was not ridiculing true honor, but he was putting into the mouth of this comic fat man satire of toplofty and overblown sentiments so often expressed by pompous men. To realistic Jack Falstaff, in imminent danger of being run through with a sword, fine words and fine sentiments took second place to safety. And because we have listened to too much high-flown oratory expressing exalted but insincere sentiments, we laugh at Falstaff's renunciation of the abstract forms of honor.

Another passage that displays the earthy humor of Falstaff—and Shakespeare's capacity for the nuance of the right phrase and precise concrete detail—may be worth recalling from *The Merry Wives of Windsor*. Falstaff, you recall, had taken refuge in a large basket of dirty laundry when surprised by Mistress Ford's husband; the servants had then taken the laundry to the Thames to be washed and had dumped Falstaff in the river. He is later reporting this indignity to his friend Bardolph: "Have I lived to be carried in a basket, like a barrow of butcher's offal, and to be thrown in the Thames? Well, if I be served such another trick, I'll have my brains ta'en out and buttered, and give them to a dog for a New Year's gift. The rogues slighted me into the river with as little remorse as they would have drowned a blind bitch's puppies, fifteen i' the litter; and you may know by my size that I have a kind of alacrity in sinking. If the bottom were as deep as hell, I should down. I had been drowned but that the shore was shelvy and shallow—a death that I abhor, for the water swells a man, and what a thing should I have been when I had been swelled! I should have been a mountain of mummy" (III.v. 4–18).

The seeming incapacity of so many writers of our time to comprehend the importance, and the value, of humor in literature is a cultural calamity. Falstaffian humor, of course, is not the only kind that we should cherish. I am merely using Falstaff as the "symbol"—heaven forgive the word—for the amusement and gaiety that our greatest dramatist and poet believed desirable in his writing.

Humor is a solvent of social and cultural ills. Since that is so, we particularly need it in our times. But, you say, these are grievous and terrifying days, and we find nothing funny in our lives. We must treat with deadly seriousness all our problems. It is blasphemous to laugh in the presence of injustice, inequality, poverty, pain, and distress.

Yet our distant ancestors of Shakespeare's age suffered more than we suffer, stood in greater peril than we know, endured greater injustice, inequality, and poverty than anyone today can conceive of. Yet they had the courage to face life without flinching, with laughter on their lips. Most Elizabethans had no choice except to stay within the narrow limits of the status to which they were born, yet they did not grow psychopathic from frustration. Poverty was acute, but nobody had yet thought of that most corrosive of all political lies, the shoddy promise that government will end it.

Let us remember that Shakespeare was given us both to delight and to instruct—but not to instruct with the sour attitude of the schoolmaster. And let us pray that dramatic producers will give us his plays without inserting any lessons of their own invention for our salvation. We may be too unregenerate to be saved—at least by a distorted Shakespeare.

VII

The Renaissance Tradition
of Science and the Humanities

THOUGHTFUL MEN are troubled by the state of learning in the world that we have inherited. Some pessimists gloomily predict a return to the Dark Ages, to a world that will care as little about learning as did Europe before the rise of the monks of Cluny in the tenth century. Learning, others point out, has become so specialized and fractionalized that the humanist can no longer comprehend science and the scientist has no time for humanism. In attempting to imitate the methods of the scientist, the humanist is accused of reducing the humanities to an arid desert without meaning to the generality of men.

Perhaps we might profitably consider for a moment the ideals of humanistic learning in the early Renaissance, when men rediscovered the values of the classical world and attempted to apply them to life in the fifteenth and sixteenth centuries. Our own lives are infinitely more complicated, to be sure, than were the lives of the men of the Renaissance, or at least we think so, but humanistic values of that earlier age still have validity for us if we can understand them aright. We particularly need to realize the unity of learning, scientific and humanistic. We cannot live successfully in two worlds. All of us, as best we can, must attempt to comprehend, if not the technicalities, at least the implications of both worlds. Indeed, it is my observation that some scientists are also excellent humanists, and the latter ought to make more of an effort to comprehend the world of science, as did the men of the Renaissance.

Our world at this particular stage in history is peculiar and puzzling. As parents sometimes say of children, perhaps we are merely going through a "phase," but it is unlike any phase that history has previously recorded. For the first time, the elders in sophisticated society, the elders of the more educated groups, seem bent on abandoning their inheritance. With the precipitate haste that the Belgians displayed when they left the Congo, our sophisticated elders are fleeing responsibility and proclaiming the wisdom and divinity of youth. They give every evidence of bad conscience. Because they have been unable to insure the millennium, they would abandon their mistakes to a younger generation whose ignorance and inexperience are sufficient to give them both arrogance and assurance. Academic sophisticates have been especially eager to cry peccavi. Some among us would turn control over to the most virginal minds in the student body. Innocence of knowledge or experience has somehow become a virtue, particularly innocence of any taint of history or antiquity. In this we differ markedly from the men of the Renaissance. And some of our humanists, who are in the forefront of this new dispensation, would be a puzzle to their counterparts in the fifteenth century.

The fifteenth century believed in the wisdom of the ancients. We have proclaimed our freedom from the fetters of antiquity. Our ancestors thought that the accumulated wisdom of the race had certain universal values. We appear to believe that originality and experimentation are the prime values, and that we ought not be handicapped by any encrustations of knowledge from the past. So youth disdains the classics and concentrates on emanations from the most recent authors who happen to be fashionable at the moment, in the belief that if a writer is modern he is also "relevant," one of the most abused and most misunderstood words in the language. Unhappily, what is "relevant" at noon today may not be relevant at 3:00 P.M. tomorrow. The humanists of the Renaissance differed from us in this respect because they found intense relevance in classical literature, and they made practical use of the classics in everyday life. I shall provide illustrations of this below. Although the Renaissance had its share of indecent writing, it was not elevated to "relevance." Pietro Aretino, for example, wrote bawdy sonnets and dialogues, and men laughed at them, but nobody solemnly found them "significant"; yet some of our critics discover deep truths in *Portnoy's Complaint* and similar writings.

The Renaissance humanists were men of intense purpose, and their purposes were practical. They did not consider themselves an anointed priestcraft; they did not invent a special jargon of their trade; they did not write merely for one another; they did not go to conventions of their kind and spend their time in self-congratulation; particularly they did not despise the men of the marketplace and the forum. They sought to communicate to the generality of men, and their communication had a purpose, practical and utilitarian.

In our time, it has become unfashionable to apply the words *practical* and *utilitarian* to the sacred subjects of the humanities. We have subscribed to a perverse view that the humanities ought to be above and beyond ordinary usefulness. Indeed, I am afraid we have sometimes tended to believe that the humanities were too rarefied and precious for appreciation and understanding by the common herd. More recently, some of our advanced thinkers in this area would identify the common herd no longer with the unwashed (now elevated to sanctity, like the desert saints), but with what *Time* magazine calls "Middle America"—the middle class. William Shakespeare would be vastly puzzled by the attitude of certain practitioners of poetry and criticism in our time. He held extremely bourgeois views. He wanted to make money. So he wrote with one eye on the box office and carpentered his plays to attract the largest possible audience. He had a supreme sense of the theater and knew precisely what would go on the stage. These qualities did not interfere with the genius of a great poet and dramatist. Hence his plays have lived through the changing fashions of the centuries. One might note in passing that closet drama, drama written in the study for the delectation of the precious few, has never lived or exerted much influence in the world.

Many of the greatest scholars, artists, and writers of the early Renaissance were practical men, convinced that their efforts should be purposeful and should serve society, though they did not use that word. They were likely to say that they served their prince or the state.

Some of these Renaissance figures were also scientists and engineers. They suffered no delusions about the sacredness of humanistic disciplines. They applied their art to the problems of the day in as sensible a way as they knew how. And they took pride in their competence, the variety of their skills, and the breadth of their knowledge. Narrow specialization was not for them. They might insist that one or another of their accomplishments transcended the others, but they did not apologize for diverse interests. Michelangelo, for example, constantly denied that he was a painter. When Pope Julius II kept plaguing him to get on with the decoration of the Sistine Chapel, Michelangelo replied in letters always signed "Michelangelo Buonarroti, Sculptor."

In a political emergency, the city of Florence discovered in humanistic learning practical values that any state might envy. Once more Florence proved that the pen is more powerful than the sword, but it was the pen of writers in republican Rome. In the year 1399, Giangaleazzo Visconti, duke of Milan, was besieging Florence. He planned to add the Florentine republic to the empire that he was trying to weld together in northern Italy. As a republic, Florence was held in suspicion by other city-states ruled by despots, and Florence needed allies. It also needed doctrines that would encourage its own citizens to hold out against the Milanese soldiers. Florentine scholars found the propaganda the city needed in the works of Cicero and Sallust, whose ringing defenses of liberty echoed from that earlier republic whence Florence traced its own beginnings. Thanks to Latin propaganda—and the fortunate death of Giangaleazzo, on September 3, 1402—Florence preserved its freedom.

One of the most famous educators of Renaissance Italy—and one of the great educational figures of the world—was Vittorino da Feltre, a humanist whose teachings remain valid to this day. Better than any other figure of the fifteenth century, Vittorino demonstrated the infinite utility of humane learning. A graduate of the University of Padua, he left a professorship there because of the riotous students—a familiar note—and went to Venice, where he set up a school of his own. Learned in mathematics, Latin, and Greek, Vittorino sought to adapt the past to the uses of the present. He did not conceive of the scholar as one who had retired to a life of contemplation. The scholar owed a debt to society and he paid it by teaching others to lead useful and active lives. In other words, Vittorino by precept and example showed that the scholar was a public-spirited and patriotic citizen, and he had no patience with the notion that scholarship gave any man the right to remain aloof from the ordinary obligations of society. But he did not go to the opposite extreme. He insisted that the scholar should serve society in accordance with his special competence, and not pretend to competence in areas where he had none.

In the 1420s, Gianfrancesco Gonzaga, marquis of Mantua, was looking for a scholar to establish a school where his own children could be properly educated. Hearing of the fame of Vittorino's school in Venice, Gonzaga offered him a post in Mantua. Vittorino was happy at Venice and made hard terms. But at last he agreed to come to Mantua. "I accept the post, on this understanding only," he wrote the marquis, "that you require from me nothing which shall be in any way unworthy of either of us; and I will continue to serve you so long as your own life shall command respect." [1] Vittorino remained in Mantua until his death, twenty-three years later, in 1446.

The school that he established gained fame throughout Italy. At his insistence, the marquis subsidized poor but talented scholars and permitted him to accept students whom Vittorino regarded as promising from other princely houses of Italy. Vittorino believed in strict discipline, and if a young prince proved worthless, out he went. One of his most worthy princelings was Federigo, later Duke of Urbino, who to the end of his days remembered Vittorino as a master deserving

[1] Eugene F. Rice, Jr., ed., *Vittorino da Feltre and Other Humanist Educators*, by William Harrison Woodward (New York, 1963), p. 24.

infinite respect. To Vittorino's teaching this most feared of the condottieri (professional soldiers who sold their services to the highest bidder) owed the inspiration that made him one of the greatest patrons of learning and the arts of his time.

Vittorino was only one of many great humanistic teachers. Others could be mentioned who had the same ideals, men who taught that learning should develop all sides of man's personality, that it should serve some practical purpose, and that the learned man had an obligation to serve the state to the best of his abilities. That did not mean leading a violent crew of wreckers to break the windows of the marquis of Mantua's palace, for example.

Another great teacher was Guarino da Verona, whose son Battista wrote in 1459 a treatise, *Upon the Method of Teaching and of Reading the Classical Authors*. Both father and son believed that an educated man had to know Latin and Greek, for these two classical tongues opened vast storehouses of learning and wisdom. Battista Guarino quoted Alexander the Great on the value of a worthy teacher: "Thus the instinct of Alexander of Macedon was a sound one which led him to say that, whilst he owed to his father Philip the gift of life, he owed to his tutor Aristotle an equal debt, namely the knowledge how to use it." Emphasizing the necessity of avoiding a wrong choice in a teacher, Battista declared that a teacher should have good manners.[2] The emphasis on courtesy runs throughout the educational writings of the time. Violence in manners, barbaric behavior, the humanists taught, marked a man as uneducated and unfit to take a place as a counselor to his prince.

Aeneas Sylvius Piccolomini, later Pope Pius II, in a treatise written as a letter to the young king of Bohemia and Hungary in 1450, commended classical philosophy as a source of wisdom for the education of a gentleman—and he insisted that a leader as well as a teacher ought to be a gentleman. "Respect towards women, affection for children and for home; pity for the distressed, justice towards all; self-control

[2] Ibid., p. 162.

in anger, restraint in indulgence, forbearance in success; contentment, courage, duty—these are some of the virtues to which philosophy will lead you," he asserted.[3] To achieve these virtues, he commended especially the study of all the works of Cicero, among other classical authors. Most important of Cicero's essays, he considered, were the treatises on old age and friendship. An earlier generation in this country looked on Cicero's *De senectute* as a source of wisdom which the young were enjoined to read either in the Latin original or in translation. Nowadays, this treatise on the wisdom of the ancients would doubtless be regarded as heretical if any of this generation had ever heard of it.

Men of the Renaissance did not restrict their definition of humanists merely to professional specialists in linguistics and classical letters. They prized diversity of learning and skills, and they included as humanists the great architects and artists who demonstrated their knowledge of classical learning and of the new science then developing. The division of mankind into two worlds, one of science and one of letters, in the manner of Sir Charles Snow, would have been unthinkable in this age.

One of the greatest of the early Renaissance architects, Filippo Brunelleschi, who completed the Duomo in Florence by erecting the enormous dome that others had thought impossible, made no pretense of being a man of letters, yet he was the intellectual associate of learned men of his time and was by way of being a literary scholar in such spare time as he could find. He learned geometry from the cosmographer and physician, Paolo Toscanelli, who influenced Columbus. Making himself a careful student of Dante, he took part in learned discussions of that poet and of Christian doctrine illustrated in the *Divine Comedy*. According to Giorgio Vasari, Toscanelli was so impressed with Brunelleschi's expositions that "he thought he was listening to a new St. Paul."[4] Brunelleschi found time for these intellectual activities while he was designing and supervising the erection of

[3] Ibid., pp. 157–58.
[4] Giorgio Vasari, *The Lives of the Painters, Sculptors, and Architects*, 4 vols. (London, 1963), 2:272.

the dome of the Duomo, designing the marvelous Pazzi Chapel, and busying himself with other strictly professional duties.

One of the brilliant Renaissance humanists who is not well enough known to English-speaking peoples is Leon Battista Alberti, truly a Renaissance man as we understand that synonym for versatility. Born in Venice in 1404, son of an exiled Florentine, Alberti grew up among artists and intellectuals, but he never lost contact with the ordinary man in the street. Indeed, that is one of the characteristics of Renaissance Italians. Steeped in Latin literature, probably taught by the famous Latin humanist Gasparino da Barzizza at Milan, Alberti early demonstrated his literary ability. When a student at the University of Bologna, he wrote a comic piece in Latin, attributed to an ancient Roman, one Lepidus, whose work Alberti claimed to have discovered in an old manuscript. It was written so well that it fooled the great printer Aldus Manutius, who published it as a newly discovered classic. From this time onward, Alberti was recognized for his wit and learning, as well as for his many skills. One of a small group of brilliant spirits whom Lorenzo the Magnificent brought together at a summer resort for conversation, Alberti outshone them all. His writings were numerous and varied: comic pieces of satire; treatises on the art of love, on the tranquillity of the soul, on the law, on the qualities of his dog, and on horsebreeding; amorous verses; serious treatises on painting, sculpture, architecture, politics, and the government of a family; and an Italian grammar. In fact his grammar of the Italian language has been described as "the first modern grammar of a living European language." [5] And he proved his own abilities in the practice of more than one craft: artist, sculptor, architect, and engineer.

In 1441 we find Alberti in Florence, organizing a public contest among poets. As a philosopher, he cast his influence on the side of the active rather than the contemplative life,

[5] Leon Battista Alberti, *The Family in Renaissance Florence. A Translation of I Libri della Famiglia by Leon Battista Alberti*, trans. Renée Neu Watkins (Columbia, S.C., 1969), p. 7.

but the activism of Alberti and the other humanists of his time was constructive rather than destructive. Although these men were aware of the shortcomings of society and the iniquities of governments, they did not seek to destroy but to correct and rebuild. The dignity of man could be achieved, Alberti maintained, in work and only in work. Every man should have a calling and labor in it, each according to his abilities, he insisted. This was common doctrine in this period and persisted down to recent times. Only in our time has the virtue of work for its own sake been called into question.

Lest we dismiss Alberti as a mere dilettante with time to write a shelfful of books expounding his views, let us remember that he was the architect of the Tempio Malatestiana in Rimini, of the facade of Santa Maria Novella in Florence, of the Palazzo and Loggia Rucellai in Florence, of the churches of San Sebastiano and San Andrea in Mantua, and of many other buildings. His treatise of architecture, *De re aedificatoria*, written in Latin and translated into Italian and many other languages, had a lasting influence. Though Alberti went back to the Roman architect Vitruvius for inspiration, he based many of his observations on actual measurements that he himself had made among the surviving classical structures in Rome.

Few men of his time better illustrated the union of both the active and the contemplative life than Alberti, but, obviously, the active, the constructively active, predominated. Alberti bore his share of a citizen's responsibilities. Vasari praised him for uniting theory and practice: "But when theory and practice are united in one person, the ideal condition is attained, because art is enriched and perfected by knowledge, the opinions and writings of learned artists having more weight and more credit than the words or works of those who have nothing more to recommend them beyond what they have produced, whether it be done well or ill. The truth of these remarks is illustrated by Leon Battista Alberti, who, having studied the Latin tongue and practiced architecture, perspective, and painting, has left works to which modern artists can add nothing, although numbers of them have surpassed him in practical skill." [6]

Devotion to the humanities and a recognition of their value to society were not confined to professional scholars or to brilliant geniuses like Leon Battista Alberti. Few more devoted humanists could be found in all Italy than Federigo da Montefeltro, Duke of Urbino, who lived between the years 1422 and 1482. Most famous of the condottieri, Federigo was also a learned man, a patron of artists and writers, who made the court of Urbino virtually an academy. His fame as a soldier was so great that Venice once paid him 80,000 ducats just to stay at home when that city was waging war against Ferrara. His love of books was so great that he employed the leading bookman of the age, Vespasiano da Bisticci, as his collector and had between thirty and forty copyists duplicating manuscripts for his library, for he would not tolerate a printed book among these works, beautifully bound in crimson and silver. His books eventually went to the Vatican Library. Federigo employed five men whose duty it was to read aloud to him at meals. Learned in Latin literature himself, he never forgot the teachings of his master, Vittorino da Feltre. He even had his portrait painted in full armor, reading a book. To his son Guidobaldo he passed on his love of letters, and it was Guidobaldo's court that Baldassare Castiglione described in *Il Libro del cortegiano*, translated into English by Sir Thomas Hoby in 1561 as *The Book of the Courtier*. Few books of the Renaissance had such a civilizing influence as Castiglione's and did so much to transmit humanistic ideals. Some of the early settlers of colonial America brought *The Book of the Courtier* with them so that they might have the best guide to conduct becoming a gentleman.

Federigo da Montefeltro was an eminently practical man, himself interested in science and engineering as well as the humanities. His scientific study of artillery—and the application of his learning in this field—made him the foremost soldier of his generation. The mathematics Federigo learned

[6] Vasari, *Lives* 1:346.

from Vittorino, along with his Latin and Greek, made the artillery of Urbino feared and envied throughout Italy. Federigo could see no divorce between science and the humanities. In his concept, and in that of learned men of his time, the two went together.

The best-remembered genius of the Renaissance is of course Leonardo da Vinci, whose diversity of intellectual interests has excited wonder from his own time to ours. Though Leonardo's qualities are well known, we can well afford to devote a few moments to the contemplation of the vast range of this man's learning and the way he applied his learning to practical problems. The painter of the Mona Lisa thought of himself less as an artist than as an engineer, an experimental scientist, and a research student. His research in anatomy, for example, was so thorough and discerning that medical historians devote almost as much space to Leonardo's discoveries in human anatomy as they do to those of Vesalius.

Painter, sculptor, writer, architect, physicist, botanist, geologist, paleontologist, zoologist, anatomist, and engineer, Leonardo placed art last on his list of accomplishments. When writing to Lodovico Sforza, duke of Milan, to seek employment, he placed engineering first among his qualifications, and became Lodovico's military engineer. He built fortresses, dams, and canals. An artilleryman at heart, he improved the rapidity of fire by inventing a breech-loading cannon and a prototype of the machine gun. When Milan fell to the French in 1499—in spite of Leonardo's engineering— he returned to Florence and in 1502 took service with Cesare Borgia, who named him his "engineer-general." Incidentally, Leonardo, like Machiavelli, admired Cesare Borgia because he believed that Borgia had the strength and ability to unite the warring city-states of Italy and weld them into a nation. Unfortunately, Borgia disappointed his admirers and fell a victim to his own wickedness.

Leonardo was a very modern man, indeed, and turned his talents to town planning and the problems of pollution. For the duke of Urbino he drew up a plan for sewage disposal.

We do not often think of the painter of the Last Supper on the walls of the refectory of Santa Maria delle Grazie as an engineer busy with the layouts of sewer systems. After an outbreak of the plague in Milan, he recommended to Lodovico Sforza a program for population dispersal into satellite towns.

For Florence, beset by floods, he recommended a canal to divert the waters of the Arno into a freight-carrying waterway to the sea. To overcome the problems of the hilly terrain between Florence and the Mediterranean, he proposed to tunnel the hills, and he devised boring tools for the purpose. Unfortunately, the Florentine authorities, deciding the cost would be too great, left the Arno uncurbed. If Leonardo's advice had been taken, Florence might have been spared the flood that we so vividly remember.

During the last phase of his life Leonardo was the guest of King Francis I of France and lived at Cloux; we will be in error if we think of the artist during this period as sitting before an easel painting. Actually he was busy with his own research and with practical problems: architectural designs and his royal patron's pet projects for canals. Leonardo was a great artist and a great humanist, but he applied his learning and his art to practical problems of the world around him. In his notebooks he once wrote, "Thou, O God, dost sell unto us all good things at the price of labor," and again he noted this sentiment: "Shun those studies in which the work that results dies with the worker." [7] Here was a humanist who thought constructively. If society in Leonardo's time was imperfect, he at least would do his part to improve it rather than tear it down.

Only a little less behind Leonardo in versatility was Michelangelo, sculptor, painter, architect, and poet. Always a modest man, Michelangelo stoutly denied that he was a painter. On more than one occasion he wrote, "I am no painter." Yet this was the artist who spent four long years

[7] William B. Parsons, *Engineers and Engineering in the Renaissance* (Baltimore, 1939), p. 22.

98

painting the magnificent frescoes of the Sistine Chapel that today are the wonder of the world.

After the sack of Rome in 1527 by the troops of the Emperor Charles V, Michelangelo was employed by Florence as military engineer to fortify the hill of San Miniato. The sculptor of the David did an equally superb job of building forts on the hill overlooking Florence.

Like Leonardo, Michelangelo studied anatomy from dissections, and he told Vasari that he regretted that he could not write a treatise on the subject, but modesty about his skill of expression prevented. Vasari remarks, however, that Michelangelo always "clearly expressed his ideas in a few words," certainly a virtue in a prolix age. "He was very fond of reading the Italian poets," Vasari continued, "especially Dante, whom he much admired and whose ideas he adopted. Petrarch was also a favorite author of his, and he delighted in composing serious madrigals and sonnets upon which commentaries have since been made." Vasari mentions a lecture on one of Michelangelo's sonnets delivered before the Florentine Academy, and the poetic exchanges between Michelangelo and his great friend Vittoria Colonna, marchesa of Pescara.

Michelangelo had a satirical sense of humor that his contemporaries did not always appreciate. In painting the Last Judgment in the Sistine Chapel, he inserted the portrait of a pompous papal official as a devil in hell. When the official complained to Pope Paul III and demanded that he be removed from his undignified pose, the pope smiled and replied that if Michelangelo had pictured him in purgatory he might have intervened, but the pope had no jurisdiction over hell.

Michelangelo, again like Leonardo, had a bourgeois respect for money and saw to it that he was well paid for his services. But he was exceedingly generous and gave away thousands of ducats to deserving friends. Most of the great artists saw to it that they were well paid. An exception to the rule was Donatello, who was so careless of money that he kept his cash in a basket suspended by a cord from the ceiling of his studio. Cosimo de' Medici, concerned about Donatello's carelessness, left instructions in his will that his executors were to see that the improvident sculptor did not suffer.

As a poet, Michelangelo enjoyed a contemporary reputation that placed him in the first rank as a man of letters. But he was invariably modest about his literary accomplishments. In his old age he sent a sonnet to Vasari that tells of his melancholy:

> Arrived already is my life's brief course,
> Through a most stormy sea, in a frail bark,
> At mankind's common port and at the shores
> Where one accounts for one's deeds, bright or dark.
> O now I know how foolish and how stark
> My art has been, so far from its true source,
> And how I made an idol and a monarch
> Of something that, alas, gives but remorse.
>
> Of all my thoughts of love, once gay and light,
> What will now be, if two deaths I'm near?
> Of the first I am sure, the second I dread.
> Painting no more, nor sculpture, can now quiet
> My soul, turned to that Love divine that, here,
> To take us, opened its arms on a cross and bled.[8]

Michelangelo combined those traits of humanism that the philosophers so often discussed, the contemplative and the active life. Although he loved solitude, he never withdrew from the world and retired within himself. He participated in the affairs of his time, spending his last years in the active supervision of the rebuilding of St. Peter's in Rome. He spent his strength and his eyesight painting the ceiling of the Sistine Chapel; he built effective forts on San Miniato to protect Florence; in the meantime he wrote moving sonnets to Vittoria Colonna. Here was a humanist who achieved supreme greatness and never let arrogance spoil his sense of values.

[8] *The Complete Poems of Michelangelo*, trans. Joseph Tusiani (London, 1960), pp. 151–52.

Among the learned humanists of the fifteenth and early sixteenth centuries were several distinguished physicians. One of these was an Englishman, Thomas Linacre, who received his medical degree at Padua and spent several years in Italy absorbing the new learning, especially Greek. In Florence he was welcomed by Lorenzo the Magnificent and permitted to share with two Medici princes instruction in Greek. One of the young Medici, Giovanni, later became Pope Leo X. Linacre carried back to England an enthusiasm for Greek and Latin learning; for the rest of his life he pursued a career as physician to Henry VII and Henry VIII, and combined the practice of medicine with the teaching of Greek. Thomas More learned his Greek from Linacre, and Erasmus, when he came to England, sat at his feet. Linacre also wrote in two fields and achieved a reputation for learning from both his grammatical and his medical works. Thomas Fuller called him the "restorer of learning," and others have believed that Browning had him in mind when he wrote "The Grammarian's Funeral." [9] His translations of Galen's medical treatises from Greek into Latin gave European physicians the most accurate versions of the Greek physician's work they had yet possessed.

Among the Renaissance medical humanists, we ought to remember François Rabelais, who satirized pedantry but was himself a man of vast learning and the translator of Hippocrates' aphorisms into Latin.

Another important medical humanist of the Renaissance was Girolamo Fracastoro of Verona, physician, physicist, astronomer, geologist, and poet. He recognized the significance of fossils, was probably the first scientist to discuss the magnetic poles, and chose Latin poetry as the means of discussing the diagnosis and treatment of syphilis. Few other physicians have grown lyrical to this extent in writing technical papers. Fracastoro's *Syphilis sive morbus gallicus*, published in Venice in 1530, gave the name by which this disease has since been known. Fracastoro, usually Latinized

[9] Fielding H. Garrison, *An Introduction to the History of Medicine* (Philadelphia and London, 1960), p. 195.

to Fracastorius, was a genius in advance of his time, a humanist of vast learning, and a physician with discriminating insights; for example, he suspected that infections were caused by microorganisms.[10]

The tradition of humanist physicians has extended from the Renaissance to our own time. The Johns Hopkins University—and the Tudor and Stuart Club founded by Sir William Osler—has included many excellent humanists among its distinguished physicians. Despite the tremendous burden of keeping up with their own professional literature, medical doctors have frequently been men of letters.

The humanistic philosophers of the Renaissance gave a great impetus to scientific research when they emphasized the omnipresence of God in nature. Pico della Mirandola, disciple of Marsilio Ficino, the great Platonist, helped to reconcile Christianity and Platonism and to popularize the idea of the goodness of the universe. Ficino, one might note, was also a physician. Since God's world was good, men had a moral right, even an obligation, to study the beneficence of the Creator in providing man with so much that was both good and desirable. With such justification, investigators turned to examine the physical world around them, and the spirit of scientific research was born.

If the Italian humanists needed encouragement for their ideal of versatility, they received it from the example of Lorenzo de' Medici, "the Magnificent." The head of a great international banking house, the leader of the oligarchy that really ruled Florence, Lorenzo had time to be a poet and a student of the classics. He also concerned himself with such practical matters as the improvement of dairy cattle, the development of a botanical garden, and the breeding of race horses. An architect himself of no mean ability, he submitted a design for the completion of the cathedral of Florence in competition with some of the greatest artists and architects of the day. A profound student of the classics, Lorenzo was the patron of scholars and the encourager of learning.[11] By

[10] Ibid., pp. 232–33.
[11] See Vincent Cronin, *The Florentine Renaissance* (New York, 1967), pp. 216–17.

precept and example he emphasized the value of the humanities to society.

We could devote vastly more space to enumerating the qualities of a multitude of humanists who shared Lorenzo's views about the obligations of the scholar to serve society. That, indeed, has been the goal of all great humanists from the Renaissance to our own time. We should not forget that many scholars in fields of the humanities have made great contributions to the well-being of mankind in the twentieth century. We should also not forget that many scientists are also humanists in their points of view and often in their attainments. Too much has been made of the separation of these two great areas of learning.

Too often in recent years, some of those who lay claim to being humanists have fallen short of their high calling and become either cynical or iconoclastic. Some have withdrawn from the world of reality and devoted themselves to the cultivation of a self-destroying guild, a kind of occult priestcraft in which they talk only to one another and write only for the understanding of the anointed. A few have even become leaders of the cult of destruction and have proclaimed a revolution, but a curious revolution that has no positive aims, merely the destruction of society as it exists.

An article in the winter issue of *American Scholar* (1969) by Kenneth Eble entitled "The Scholarly Life" concludes with an indictment of contemporary humanistic scholarship and its advocates. "The shame of humanistic study in the face of so much that needs to be done," the author asserts, "is the vast amount of learning that means little to the person doing it, little to the scholar supervising it, and nothing whatsoever to the society that supports it. Part of the scholar's task must be that of removing some of the undergrowth that scholarship has encouraged to grow up around formal study in the humanities. Another part is to make humanistic scholarship generous to attract more of the intelligence, imagination, and energy of young scholars."

Professor Eble's indictment may be too severe, but all of us who have watched the progress of humanistic scholarship and so-called research in the humanities during the past two decades know that an enormous amount of it has no meaning and no purpose. The lack of a sense of values among the practitioners of the humanities is one of the serious problems facing the humanistic disciplines today. A scholar need not become an "activist" in the current meaning of the term, that is, a banner-carrier ready to "demonstrate" at the twitch of a whisker about matters of which he has little real knowledge. Too often that is the extent of the present-day humanist's participation in the problems of society. But modern humanists might study the role of the Renaissance humanists and see how they applied their learning in areas where they knew they could make a contribution.

A critic will at once object that no longer can a man of letters be also an artist, an architect, or a physician as could humanists in the Renaissance. Our world of learning has become too complex for such participation. But the humanistic scholar can still apply his abilities systematically to problems of education, the advancement of genuine learning, politics, and social welfare.

The student of the humanities has an opportunity to be conversant with the best that has been thought and said in the past. His discipline brings him into intimate contact with great minds, and his studies ought to induce a sense of perspective, proportion, and discrimination. For centuries men have believed that humanistic disciplines are useful in the training of leaders. Thomas Jefferson pointed out that republics are liable to fall when their supply of leaders of intelligence and character fails. He believed that a democratic society should make provisions for liberal studies to insure an adequate succession of leaders. Many generations before Jefferson, Rabelais also commended liberal studies as necessary to a well-ordered state, and he warned against those scholars who took refuge in nooks and crannies that kept them away from a full and active life. Men should not grow squint-minded, he declared, nor look out at life through a little hole.

If the professors of liberal studies do not make the most of their opportunities, if they cultivate only a small priest-craft, they will grow squint-minded. Today we need humanists who have wisdom acquired from a profound study of the best thought that has gone before, who are concerned with distilling the wisdom of the ancients and transmitting it to potential leaders. As Vittorino long ago maintained, such teachers ought to be men and women whose example would induce worthy emulation, who would emphasize the importance of character no less than learning. The humanist today has a vital role to play and he would do well to contemplate the ideals and the practice of the great minds of the Renaissance.

At the end of World War I, Sir William Osler, a great teacher of medicine and a man of liberal studies himself, surveyed the state of learning in an essay, *The Old Humanities and the New Science* (Boston, 1920), and prescribed the study of the classics for the disease of specialism that he saw overtaking education, scholarship, and science itself. In a footnote he quoted with approval the platform for a liberal education recommended by Prof. J. A. Stewart of Oxford: "No humane letters without natural science, and no natural science without humane letters." Society as a whole requires this fusion of the most significant branches of learning. Both humanists and scientists must struggle toward this end, difficult as the problem may be in an era of ever increasing complexity.

VIII

The Classics and

the Eighteenth-Century Gentleman

IN OUR OWN AGE, when it has become fashionable to disparage both the notion of the gentleman and the belief in the value of tradition, it is perhaps worthwhile to recall the value that earlier periods placed on both behavior and learning. Learning, traditionally, implied a knowledge of the literature of Greece and Rome, not for cultural decoration but for an acquaintance with the wisdom of the ancients. From the recorded experience of the past, our ancestors believed that they too might acquire a modicum of wisdom.

Recently, however, thanks to the recrudescence of decadent Rousseauism grafted on ill-understood Freudianism, we have come to believe that wisdom resides in the innocence of youth. Indeed, to observe some academic administrators scrambling to placate student rebels and to prove that they are "with it," one would believe that the best equipment for life is a tabula rasa, and the blanker the better. No longer are the elders of the tribe respected, nor is their experience prized. Instead, we have enthroned youth, put them on boards of trustees, and let them tell us what is "relevant" in learning. Along with the deification of juvenility has come a disparagement of tradition and the values formerly believed to be implicit in a knowledge of history. Sociologists have invented a language to glorify the "innovative" (a word they love) and to preach a new religion of "fresh concepts and perceptions" (again words out of their armory of jargon). This revolution has demolished the concept of the gentleman and the cultural heritage that made him what he was.

The intellectual and spiritual inheritance of the eighteenth-century gentleman derived from the Renaissance emphasis on classical culture as a civilizing force. The rediscovery of the literature of Greece and Rome in the fifteenth and sixteenth centuries, and the new interpretations put upon that literature, profoundly influenced Western civilization for centuries to come. Only in our time has there been a general movement to discredit the classics as essential to a sound education.

Although few people in a technological society such as ours would contend that the classical education that sufficed in the eighteenth century would be adequate today, it might be useful for us to examine the basis of earlier educational theory. First of all, our ancestors never doubted that the ancient civilizations of Greece and Rome produced a race of wise men who had something valuable to impart to later generations. To gain access to that store of knowledge and wisdom, they learned the classical languages. The ability to read Greek and Latin marked a man as cultivated and a candidate for polite society. If occasionally a pedant emerged from the classical curriculum, by and large the regimen produced men who knew how to mix learning and the daily routines of life in the right proportions.

The men of the eighteenth century, like their predecessors in the Renaissance, regarded classical learning as a utilitarian guide to intelligent living. Jefferson himself believed that a democratic state such as he envisioned required an *aristoi*, but an aristocracy of intelligence. For this type of leadership Jefferson believed that the wisdom of the ancients, coupled with the new scientific learning of the modern world, would be particularly valuable.

For a moment, we might contemplate the background of Jefferson's own society to see what the eighteenth-century Virginia gentleman thought about the classics. At the outset let us remember that these were eminently practical men. They suffered no nonsense about any taint that would come from trade or the labor necessary to direct the operation of tobacco plantations, the sale of the product, and the business acumen required to get ahead in the world. In short, they were no gilded cavaliers, dainty in silken neck-cloths, dancing their lives away under the magnolias, as romantic novelists have sometimes pictured them. Like all colonial

107

Americans they were hardworking men struggling to make a success in a new land far from the amenities of older civilizations. For that reason they were particularly concerned not to grow barbarous in the wilderness, a phrase that occurs more than once in their writings. One way to keep from growing barbarous was to retain a knowledge of the most civilized cultures known to them, namely, those of ancient Greece and Rome. For that reason little colonial libraries, brought over for utility, not for ornament and ostentation, frequently had, along with books on farming, horsebreeding, medicine, law, and religion, a fair share of classical authors, sometimes in the original, sometimes in translation.

One of the earliest libraries brought to Virginia was that of a preacher who did not live to practice his calling, an Anglican named John Goodborne. The library that he sent over in 1635 contained 157 works, of which 27 were by Greek or Latin authors. The subjects included poetry, plays, history, science, philosophy, oratory, and three anthologies of classical excerpts. Represented in this little library were Thucydides, Plutarch, Caesar, Justin, Suetonius, Homer, Vergil, Pindar, Ovid, Horace, Juvenal, Persius, Plautus, Terence, Seneca, Isocrates, Quintilian, and Cicero. Goodborne had also added the scientific works of Aristotle, the medical treatises of Celsus, and the natural history of Aelianus. That Goodborne, who was coming to Virginia to save the souls of the colonists and to teach them a way of life in the present world, believed that these authors were essential is significant of the seventeenth-century attitude toward the classics, an attitude that carried over into the next century and beyond.

An examination of colonial libraries, not only in Virginia but elsewhere, reveals a continuing interest in the classics. John Carter, who died in 1690, left a library of sixty-two titles including a treatise on military tactics by Aelian, which he probably thought would be useful in defending Virginia against the Indians or the Spaniards, Plutarch's *Lives* in North's translation, Chapman's translation of the *Iliad*, John Ogilby's English version of Vergil's *Works*, and translations of Ovid. Such were the books available to the children of this ancestor of the large Carter clan of Virginia. His descendants added to these classical resources in their own various libraries.

Another seventeenth-century Virginian who had a representative classical library was Col. Ralph Wormely of Rosegill. He had works both in the original language and in translation of Plutarch, Aesop, Thucydides, Vergil, Ovid, Horace, Cicero, Seneca, Terence, Lucan, and Quintus Curtius.

Throughout the eighteenth century the libraries of Virginia planters continued to show an increase in the proportion of classical authors. The best classical scholar in Virginia in the early eighteenth century was the second Richard Lee of Westmoreland County. He had an excellent classical library and went so far as to keep his farm notes in Greek, Latin, or Hebrew. A descendant wrote that he spent his whole life in study and thus "neither diminished nor improved his paternal estate." But if Richard Lee was less concerned with land-grabbing than some of his contemporaries, he did not neglect his civic duties. He was, moreover, the ancestor of one of the most distinguished families in the commonwealth.

One of Lee's intimate friends, Robert Carter of Corotoman, known because of his wealth and pride as "King" Carter, was vastly concerned that his own sons should have a proper classical education. When he sent the boys to school in England, he instructed his agent to see that they had the best possible instruction in Latin. One letter complained that he wished the boys' schoolmaster, a certain Solomon Low, "had kept in the old way of teaching the Latin tongue and had made my boys perfect in their understanding of Lilly's *Grammar* and the old school books that we and our forefathers learned. There is one book which did me the most service of any that I was acquainted with, to wit, the *Janua Linguarum Trilinguis* in Latin, English, and Greek, writ by John Comenius, the best stock of Latin words, and in the best sense to suit the genius of boys, even to their manhood, of any book that ever I met with in my life." The influence of Comenius in perpetuating classical learning on both sides of the Atlantic I have dealt with elsewhere.

The attitude of Richard Lee and Robert Carter toward the classics and the belief in their value as practical guides to life illustrate the concepts held by other members of the Virginia ruling class, then and later. To describe all of their libraries and their concern with classical authors would be tediously repetitious. I have discussed this theme in a short article, "The Classical Tradition in Colonial Virginia," *Papers of the Bibliographical Society of America* 33 (1939):85–97. But I should like to mention the devotion of William Byrd II to classical learning.

Byrd was one of Virginia's most urbane gentlemen, a frequent agent of the colony before the Board of Trade in London, a writer, and a man of the world. Furthermore he kept a diary in shorthand and wrote down his daily stint of Greek, Hebrew, or Latin, which for some thirty years he never neglected. His life extended from 1674 to 1744. Byrd's library, one of the best in the colonies, had a large collection of classical works that he constantly used.

A passage from his diary, picked at random, reveals his routine reading of the classics. This is for October 31, 1709: "I rose at 6 o'clock and read two chapters in Hebrew and some Greek in Lucian. I said my prayers and ate milk for breakfast. About 10 o'clock we went to court. The committee met to receive proposals for the building [of] the College and Mr. Tullitt undertook it for £2,000 provided he might [get] wood off the College land and all assistance from England to come at the College's risk. We sat in court till 4 o'clock and then I rode to Green Springs to meet my wife. I found her there and had the pleasure to learn that all was well at home, thanks be to God. There was likewise Mrs. Chiswell. I ate boiled beef for supper. Then we danced and were merry till about 10 o'clock. I neglected to say my prayers but had good health, good thoughts, and good humor thanks be to God Almighty."

The daily exercises in Greek and Hebrew he maintained

throughout his adult life, as entries in his diaries prove. A cultivated gentleman of the early eighteenth century was expected to know the classical tongues. Hebrew was also regarded as important for the man who expected to be known for his learning, for it was the key to religious instruction as Greek and Latin were the keys to secular scholarship.

The eighteenth-century gentleman took an acquaintance with Greek and Latin for granted and was regarded as uncultivated if he did not recognize a quotation from a classical author. It was also fashionable to quote tags of Latin and the sayings of Greek philosophers and orators.

William Byrd had more than a bowing acquaintance with the best of classical writers, for he constantly read them. Although Greek and Hebrew were his normal prebreakfast fare, as his diaries indicate, he frequently read some Latin author or something in Italian or French. This regimen is indicative of the premium that a member of the eighteenth-century ruling class put on learning—and the cultivation that he believed would accrue from reading ancient writers.

We should also remember that Byrd and others of his class were not professional scholars but men of the world, busy with personal and public affairs. Yet as preoccupied as they were with a wide variety of mundane matters, they took time to acquaint themselves with the great store of literature from Greece and Rome.

The illustrations of classical interest on the part of eighteenth-century gentlemen that I have been giving are from Virginia, because Virginia in the colonial period produced a remarkable body of planter-aristocrats who consciously modeled themselves on the English landed gentry. But other regions also produced gentlemen equally interested in classical learning. In 1963 Richard M. Gummere published *The American Colonial Mind and the Classical Tradition*, in which he pointed out the widespread use of the classics by leading colonial figures.

Few professional scholars could match the classical learning of James Logan (1674–1751) of Philadelphia, an important member of the ruling hierarchy of Pennsylvania.

Although burdened with governmental problems, Logan, like Byrd, kept up his study and reading of Greek and Roman authors. He even took time to translate and publish, in 1735, *Dicta catonis;* and in 1744 he published his translation in graceful English of Cicero's *De senectute.* He was a master of Latin prose and sometimes wrote verse in Latin. Logan had perhaps the best classical library in colonial America.

In his book Gummere indicates some of the ideas that colonials got from classical authors. For example, from Thucydides they learned that the Greek colonies were independent of the mother state and owed it nothing except "sentiment and loyalty" in spirit. This idea the colonists were later to make use of in their arguments with Great Britain. Later, in debates at the Constitutional Convention of 1787, the former colonists were constantly referring to the Greek city-states and to their amphictyonic councils.

A quotation from Gummere might be enlightening about this later use of the classics by leaders in the new nation. Speaking of the influence of Greek and Roman precedents, he noted: "From Paris Jefferson shipped copies of Polybius and sets of ancient authors to Madison, a former graduate student of John Witherspoon's at Princeton, and to George Wythe, a finished Greek and Latin scholar who 'could hardly refrain from giving a line from Horace the force of an Act of Assembly.'" Gummere adds: "The debates before, during, and after the Convention of 1787 can be better understood if the doctrines of three ancient authorities—Aristotle, Cicero, and Polybius—are first clarified in relation to the establishment of the Federal government. Their testimony underlies all the suggested patterns of the new republic."

Aristotle's discussion of more than 100 constitutions was frequently quoted. Polybius supplied information, parallels, and warnings in his description of the Greek city-states. Alexander Hamilton, for instance, found in the history of the city-states, especially their constant warring with each other, lessons for his country on the necessity of union.

Plato was usually omitted from consideration by the fathers of the country because he was unrealistic and imprac-

112

tical. His *Republic* appealed to the spiritual rather than the practical aspects of man's governance. Elbridge Gerry put it succinctly when he said, "Plato was not a republican."

During the great controversies of the late eighteenth century, when colonists were arguing against what they interpreted as the oppression of the mother country, they constantly invoked classical authorities. This subject has been treated in some detail by Charles F. Mullett in his "Classical Influences on the American Revolution," *The Classical Journal* 35 (1939–40):92–104.

The Greeks most often cited by the colonials in support of their revolutionary position were Thucydides, Aristotle, Polybius, and Plutarch. If anything, Roman writers were even more popular. Cicero's *De officiis* and his orations against Catiline were constantly quoted. Mullett comments that "of the Romans, Cicero and Tacitus took first place in colonial idealization, although a considerable number of others afford additional ballast to the revolutionary contentions." Most of the favorites were writers who glorified republican Rome.

The colonials who carried on the controversies with Great Britain, at least those who wrote pamphlets and tracts quoting Greek and Roman authorities, were members of the ruling class who can be classified as gentlemen. In their formal education and in their informal reading they had steeped themselves in classical lore, and their regard for Greek and Roman precedents came as naturally to them as does our familiarity with the opinions of newspaper columnists.

One of the best examples of the influence of the classics on a seminal mind of the eighteenth century is of course Thomas Jefferson. To his father, Peter Jefferson, Thomas owed his early classical training. Peter Jefferson left, when he was dying, instructions that his son was to be given the best classical training available. By the age of nine, Thomas had begun the study of Latin, Greek, and French. Not least of the influences on Jefferson was his close association with his great teacher of law, George Wythe, who was equally well known in Virginia for his learning in Greek and Latin.

Writing to Joseph Priestly in 1800, Jefferson remarked:

"To read the Latin and Greek authors in their originals is a sublime luxury; . . . I enjoy Homer in his own language infinitely beyond Pope's translation of him, . . . I thank on my knees him who directed my early education for having put into my possession this rich source of delight; and I would not exchange it for anything which I could then have acquired and have not since acquired."

The literature of antiquity, Jefferson learned as a student, was the ultimate source of both delight and instruction—a precept that George Wythe would have given him if he had not already gleaned it from Horace. But it would be a mistake to assume that the Albemarle youth, like an eighteenth-century type of Browning's grammarian, devoted himself to the past with the zeal of a specialist. The tradition that he had inherited, a tradition developed in the sixteenth century, emphasized a well-rounded education and an amateur standing in a number of useful and ornamental arts. Balance and symmetry were important, and Jefferson, consciously or unconsciously, followed this Renaissance theory of education which gave him an enormous curiosity about a variety of things and contributed to the development of his many-sided personality. But from the classics Jefferson believed that he had obtained the basis of an ethical and philosophical system as well as the means of satisfying his aesthetic longings.

The respect for the classics acquired in his youth Jefferson retained throughout his life, but this interest was never merely academic or pedantic. For him the literature of the ancient world had a utilitarian value of the highest importance, a value that he constantly emphasized later in his plans for public schools in Virginia and the foundation of a university. Unlike some scholars who reverence antiquity, Jefferson displayed a commonsense attitude toward classical learning. The battle of the books, which aroused the biased excitement of eighteenth-century protagonists of ancient or modern learning, had no interest for Jefferson. All learning had its proper place, and he was not concerned to elevate one school over another. Both the ancients and the moderns were essential in their particular spheres.

A letter that Jefferson wrote to his nephew Peter Carr from Paris on August 19, 1785, provides a significant view of his conception of the place of the classics in the education of a gentleman who ought to look forward to serving the state. Jefferson's opinions sound like those of Vittorino da Feltre or another of the humanist educators of the Renaissance in Italy. One finds the same insistence on the development of the complete man, the necessity of exercise and physical development, the advantages of literary learning—not as an excuse for hermitlike retirement from the world but as a means of service to the state—and, lastly, the practical utility of classical authors as guides and counselors. The letter is too long to quote here *in extenso*, but a few sentences are pertinent: "For the present," Jefferson wrote, "I advise you to begin a course of ancient history, reading everything in the original and not in translations. First read Goldsmith's history of Greece. . . . Then take up ancient history in detail, reading the following books in the following order: Herodotus, Thucydides, Xenophontis Anabasis, Arrian, Quintus Curtius, Diodorus Siculus, Justin. This shall form the first stage of your historical reading and is all I need mention to you now. The next will be of Roman history: Livy, Sallust, Caesar, Cicero's epistles, Suetonius, Tacitus, Gibbon. . . . In Greek and Latin poetry you have read or will read at school Virgil, Terence, Horace, Anacreon, Theocritus, Homer, Euripides, Sophocles. . . . In morality, read Epictetus, Xenophontis Memorabilia, Plato's Socratic dialogues, Cicero's philosophies, Antoninus, and Seneca." Jefferson then advises adequate exercise, for "a strong body makes a strong mind." He recommends hunting and walking, but no ballgames. "Games played with the ball, and others of that nature, are too violent for the body and stamp no character on the mind."

Great as was Jefferson's admiration for the Greeks, he felt more at home with Roman historians and moralists. Writing to a granddaughter on December 8, 1808, he commended her program of reading and observed: "Tacitus I consider the first writer in the world without a single exception. His book is a compound of history and morality of which we have no other example."

It is not my concern here to repeat what I have written at some length elsewhere on Jefferson and the classics, but I should note in passing that he, like other of his contemporaries, took a dim view of Plato. Jefferson found him mystical, foggy, and full of fantastical whimsies. In a long letter to John Adams on July 4, 1814, he condemned Plato for his sophistries. Elsewhere he attributed to "Platonizing Christians" the confusion and misinterpretation of the simple teachings of Jesus.

Jefferson, like other gentlemen of the eighteenth century, found in the classics a vitality and a utility that justified the time spent on them. Although Jefferson advised against looking backward instead of forward, he was conscious of being the heir of all the past, and he treasured that legacy.

The men of the eighteenth century drew on classical sources for both inspiration and guidance. They believed that leaders in society had an obligation to be informed — and, if possible, to be wise. Clarity of thought and expression, and breadth of vision, were ideals to be sought. In the attainment of these ideals, the literature of Greece and Rome provided unparalleled resources. To these men, some of whom became the founders of the new nation, the past was "relevant."

IX

Flight from Tradition:
The University of Absurdum

IN FEW AREAS of modern life has the flight from tradition been more dramatic than in the field of education, especially higher education. We are told that this is a period of transition, but transition to what we are not certain. The purposes and objectives of education are in a state of flux, with profound disagreements among students, faculties, administrations, and trustees. Uneasy lies the head that wears the crown of office in any college or university.

Over the years a few friends of my acquaintance in the foundation world and the field of education have amused themselves in odd moments by creating an ideally impossible university which we shall call the University of Reductio ad Absurdum, or just Absurdum for short. We established this university in Darwin, Australia, because we thought that would be a happy distance away. Whenever any of the founders of Absurdum meet, we compare notes on faculty and administrative appointments that ought to be made, and we all keep a little list of likely candidates for posts at Absurdum. During the past five years our lists have swelled enormously, and we have an increasing group of faculty members and administrators who are richly qualified for appointment to Absurdum. Newspaper interviews and published essays by the denizens of academia provide invaluable clues to possible personnel for our Australian university. The truth is that we have more qualified personnel than any university can accommodate on its faculties and administrative staffs, and we have had to adopt a grading system in order to send to Absurdum those best fitted to the immediate problems of the day. Of late we have also had to give our attention to the selection of a proper student body, because of the overabundance of students who deserve the type of training—we shall not call it education—provided at Absurdum.

When we began to populate Darwin, Australia, with academics, we thought we were creating a sort of educational sump to drain off the impossibles from institutions where they had become a problem. We filled the principal chairs with individualists, egotists, eccentrics, anarchists, cultists, and others who had publicly demonstrated their unhappiness with the institutions in which they found themselves. In some cases the institutions had also demonstrated their official unhappiness with these individuals. We felt that it would be worth foundation support to have an institution where all the misfits could go and find their own identities, the discovery of identity being one of the clichés to which they all subscribed.

When we began the establishment of the University of Absurdum, we thought we were innovators, and that the institution would be unique. We rather hoped that it would remain unique. To our astonishment, we find that we have really founded one of the universities of the future. The idiosyncrasies and absurdities of a decade ago are rapidly becoming the orthodoxies of the present. At least one would think so from reading current periodicals and assorted educational journals.

Since we have now reached a point in educational progress when the University of Absurdum can be hailed as one of our leading experimental, avant-garde educational institutions, a pioneer in all that leading young Intellectuals advocate and demand, perhaps the annual report of Chancellor Hans Miscue for the year 1968 may be of interest. With your permission I shall read excerpts from Chancellor Miscue's report, with occasional comments that I may feel impelled to interpolate.

To the Board of Visitors:

It is with a sense of immense satisfaction that I make this report of the progress of the University of Absurdum for the fiscal year 1967–68. It is regrettable that the belligerence of both faculty and students prevented the Board of Visitors' holding its June meeting on campus, but all members of the board, I feel sure, will regard the threats of violence made by faculty and students merely as the natural evolution of the democratic spirit in this idealistic institution. Although my own office was burned by students who were publicly congratulated by a Maoist member of the English department, I regard this action of the students as a salutary catharsis of frustrations. The administration has for the time being found quarters in a reinforced concrete bunker built during the last war as a place of safety from Japanese bombings. With a certain amount of refitting, the bunker will make admirable quarters for the administration in the future. I should call the Board of Visitors' attention to the need for asbestos-lined filing cases for student records if it is decided to continue the archaic practice of grading students.

At this point perhaps I should call your attention to the students' demands that all record-keeping be abandoned. They feel that it is patently unfair to provide prospective employers with records that might prejudice them against hiring students for any reason. Most of the faculty heartily support the students in this demand. They point out that complete objectivity in giving grades is impossible and that some faculty members have openly showed hostility to students who appeared in class wearing shoes and neckties. The faculty feel that even these backward bourgeoisie, who by some mischance got into Absurdum, should not be penalized because of the inevitable prejudice in grading.

The administration has given much attention during the year to what we at Absurdum are happy to call "Participatory Democracy" in the government of the institution. Indeed, we believe Absurdum is at the forefront of institutions giving students and faculty control of all branches of administration. The chancellor merely serves as a committee chairman when invited to do so. This advance to complete democracy has relieved the central administration of a heavy burden of responsibility, and we hope Absurdum is setting an example that other similar institutions will want to follow.

This highly progressive step has not been taken without a few notable changes in the curriculum and some difficulties and unresolved problems that may be of passing interest to the Board of Visitors.

Perhaps the most remarkable advance during the past year was the abandonment of physics and chemistry entirely. The students voted, with only 20 percent objecting, to throw out these subjects because of their warlike potential. One student leader proclaimed: "Chemists and physicists are the handmaidens of war. If our bourgeois, Establishment-oriented universities had not taught chemists to make napalm, we would not be burning babies in Viet Nam. The physicists are even more blameworthy, for they are teaching the pollution of the very air around us with nuclear fission. We demand that Absurdum quit abetting the warmongers and drive these vile scientists from our campus." Although some of the faculty, particularly members of the Chemistry and Physics departments, felt that this statement was somewhat extreme, the faculty, after much debate, concurred in the student decision. That concurrence was made easier by the fact that the students rioted and wrecked the laboratories beyond any possibility of rehabilitation.

After some general discussion of subjects desirable to replace chemistry and physics, the students voted, with the concurrence of the faculty, that the core subject at Absurdum should be philosophy. The definition of philosophy, they felt, could be made broad enough to suit any taste. I might call the attention of the Board of Visitors to the growing popularity of yoga at Absurdum. The administration feels that this is a highly desirable development. So long as students, and the younger faculty, can sit cross-legged in contemplation, their potential for destruction is reduced. Since the widespread adoption of yoga, we have had several whole days when not a Molotov cocktail was thrown at any building on the campus.

The Board of Visitors will be pleased to learn of the growing popularity of courses in the humanities at Absurdum, especially English and history. We at Absurdum have long since abandoned the old stereotypes formerly taught in university courses in English and history and have introduced new fields for study that the students feel have relevance for them today. Indeed, relevance has become the watchword of the humanities, *immediate* relevance. No course, the students feel (with the younger faculty concurring), should be taught which does not help them in some fashion in solving the problems of 1967–68.

The words of one of our bright young assistant professors of English, whom we imported last year from Berkeley, will provide the Board of Visitors with a clue to the younger generation's point of view: "We should not demand that our students read outmoded and outworn classics that have no immediacy for them. These works, written in a stilted language prisoned by grammar and syntax, serve merely to suffocate their minds. We want to liberate their spirits by letting them write their own thoughts, untrammeled by grammatical and syntactical fetters. Only then can they achieve free expression. Since at Aburdum we do not require courses in the so-called classics, our literary effort should be devoted to writing, and then reading the works of our own academic contemporaries."

This experiment in creating our own literature at Absurdum has produced some quite remarkable results, especially in the stream-of-consciousness vein. Some students, it is true, have complained that the revelation of the minds of their contemporaries has occasionally bored them. We have also had a problem with some of the published works, which the Australian government, though in general benevolent, has found obscene or libelous. Two students were stabbed by angry husbands after writing in complete detail about their amorous adventures with wives of younger faculty members, but misadventures like this are bound to occur in a completely free society, which we are trying to establish on our campus.

The younger historians, the Board of Visitors will be glad to learn, have demonstrated a remarkable sense of social consciousness and responsibility to the improvement of society. The whole History Department seems imbued with a deep sense of immediate relevance. The past, they are convinced, must be made to teach lessons useful in the present. "Modern society must not let old traditions, which earlier historians glorified, influence changes which are overdue," declared one of our brightest young historians, who, I am happy to say, had his training at Harvard. "The modern historian must decide what the truth ought to have been and see that his students learn only that aspect of the past." With this enlightened point of view our History Department has undertaken the rewriting of world history since the passage of the English Reform Bill of 1832. They regard anything that happened before that date as irrelevant to modern needs. "History must be used to teach what ought to be, not what actually was, because human prejudice is such that historians cannot tell what actually was," another young historian has proclaimed.

This point of view met with a certain amount of opposition from one or two older men who pointed out that the German Nazis had employed this technique and had made history mere propaganda. But the younger faculty, with the concurrence of the students, pooh-poohed this notion as old-fashioned intransigence of those opposed to social progress.

Interpolation: Some of these views may be read in more detail in the Outlook *section of the* Washington Post *for Sunday, June 30, 1968. Some of the demonstrations of the historical point of view expressed by the Absurdum faculty may be seen in any number of books emanating from reputable publishers today.* Chancellor Miscue's report continues.

The Department of Religion at Absurdum has found much common ground with the Department of Philosophy and with the other humanities. Indeed, it is a matter of congratulation to us that our religious faculty has cooperated so extensively with other departments. We feel that they are among the most advanced thinkers at Absurdum.

Outmoded morality has no place in modern life, and the freedom of the individual personality should be the goal of spiritual aspiration, the religious faculty announced in a recent manifesto. This manifesto followed the disgraceful action of the municipal authorities of Darwin in publicly charging that the university was making common brothels of its dormitories. It is true that we make no effort to police our dormitories, for our students are all responsible citizens who would not tolerate our intervention in their behavior. They also maintain that their dormitories enjoy extraterritorial privileges and should not be invaded by the Darwin police even in search of thieves and murderers. I am happy to say that our religious leaders united in organizing a demonstration that marched on the Darwin city hall to protest the charges against the university. It is unfortunate that in the melee, which the students maintain was precipitated by police brutality, three officers were so badly mauled that they are still hospitalized.

Interpolation: Documentation for the events at Absurdum are too numerous to elucidate. See Time, Newsweek, *and daily newspapers* passim *giving accounts of student riots.* Chancellor Miscue's report continues, albeit briefly.

Our creative arts departments at Absurdum are our particular pride. In painting and sculpture we excel. I should like especially to call the attention of the Board of Visitors to the prizes our resident artists have won. A notable event occurred in the spring when Nicolo Ignoto was awarded the Absurdum Faculty Prize for Painting for his view of the Darwin Town Dump, done in vigorous reds and yellows on the rear wall of the men's latrine at the local workhouse. It is a pity that so few of our citizens have the opportunity of viewing this fine example of avant-garde art.

But the greatest source of satisfaction at Absurdum is our Music Department. We have recently abandoned all conventional music in favor of electronic sound. We realize that this is highly experimental, but our music people believe this is the wave of the future. We recently had a remarkable

concert that lasted twelve hours when one of our experimentalists picked up sounds from the atmosphere and am-
plified them so that they could be heard for three blocks.
Unhappily, some of the less musically inclined citizens of
Darwin have brought action against the university for maintaining a nuisance.

Another of our brilliant experimentalists has made an
astonishing tape which she played back to the faculty at our
last meeting. The sounds are all completely natural sounds,
sounds made by human beings in the normal course of
events. Miss Maria Singularos, the musician who made this
recording, announced that she was glad to introduce a little
humor and joy into the music, and that she found the sounds
of a man belching after meals particularly diverting.

Interpolation: See the Wall Street Journal *for July 2, 1968, for
a more detailed account of this music.* Chancellor Miscue concludes:

I could continue my report by giving more details of the
exciting new developments at Absurdum, but I want to save
the Board of Visitors from boredom. I hope some day it will
be safe for them to pay another visit to the campus, but as
yet I do not advise it.

All of us here feel that we are having a part in an exciting
new advance when old, static forms of education are giving
way to fresh types of activism. By giving the students and
faculty complete control, we believe that we have achieved
the ultimate in democracy. It is true that as yet the demonstration of that democracy has taken the form of shouting
down all opposing views, and that the loudest dissenters have
carried the day, often when they were numerically a minority, but we feel that these are merely evidences of the
growing pains of a new day. I am sure the Board of Visitors
will share my joy in these events. I hope, however, that they
will see fit to vote funds for reinforcing and refitting the
fortified bunker, which the administration feels obliged to
occupy for the time being.

*Interpolation: Is Absurdum a myth? The daily papers confirm its
actuality. What of education? Ah, that is the question.*

X

Ivory Towers: A National Imperative

IN OUR TIME it has become fashionable to speak slightingly of any learned institution that does not concern itself with immediate social salvation as an ivory tower, and therefore of doubtful utility. Scientific institutes, libraries, colleges, and universities devoted to nonutilitarian research, thought, and speculation are frequently held up to ridicule by a public demanding "relevance"—whatever that may mean at the moment.

So intense is public pressure to see that every learned institution recognizes an obligation to do good by humankind —tangible and visible good, immediately perceptible—that we have seen in recent years academic administrators scrambling with undignified haste to get down in the gutter or the ghetto, "where the action is." It makes little difference that their institutions have no vocation to perform miscellaneous social services; they must demonstrate their eagerness to wash the feet of the poor.

Let it be said, however, that this urge of academicians is sometimes prompted by ukases from trustees who want to see their institutions "alive and jumping"—and sometimes in the recent past by chanting mobs of adolescent students (and frequently adolescent faculty members) demanding they know not what. For a variety of reasons institutions of learning have felt it necessary to hide the fact that they were founded for purposes other than what Francis Bacon called the relief of man's estate.

In our eager zeal to do good by the greatest number, we have often diluted what we are pleased to call education to a sort of cultural pink lemonade. Dippers of such drink may quench temporarily a few thirsts and spread a little cheer, but not even a Pierian barrel of it will provide much of permanent value. Reduction of learning to the lowest common

125

denominator, without any compensation for those who require something better, is not likely to improve society.

Some years ago a prominent politician contracted an ailment and entered Johns Hopkins Hospital for diagnosis and treatment. After examination by one of Hopkins's famous specialists, the politician looked up and inquired, "Well, doctor, what's the verdict?" "The trouble with you," the specialist answered, "is that you have been too democratic." The trouble with much of our education today is that it has become so "democratic" that anemia is reducing it to unproductive mediocrity.

The crisis is acute and is compounded by much muddy thinking. For that reason I would like for a few moments to look back at the history of our civilization to see how the conservators of learning have saved us from barbarism and provided us with viable democratic institutions.

Nobody in his right mind will cavil at our best efforts to educate and elevate the disadvantaged and the downtrodden. That has been the hope of intelligent men from the beginning of our nation, as we shall presently see. Nor is there any inclination to justify unenlightened pedantry in our learned institutions. Much that passes for learning is so much Tweedledum and Tweedledee. Academia also has its proportion of frauds. But we need to think clearly, define our terms, and not confuse education with miscellaneous charity.

One of our current problems is a fear among the alleged intelligentsia of establishing an elite. Everybody must be common and some more common than others. Actually, this phobia has created its own elitism, an arrogant elite of the Left, which glorifies a return to primitivism, getting back to what they term first principles—which frequently means uninhibited behavior garnished with dirt. This too has a long historical background, which I shall mention in a moment.

A small but vocal minority today would reject traditional values prized by Western civilization since the days of the ancient Greeks, values that emphasize the attainment of the highest quality possible in both the material and spiritual manifestations of life. This group thinks salvation will come with the Establishment's destruction, which presumably would usher in a golden age of simplicity where everyone would live on the same level in communes and dine on organic greens gathered in the woods and fields. This ideal society would be free of most institutions as we know them, especially institutions of higher learning.

In a somewhat different context, the Russian writer Alexander Solzhenitsyn, in his novel *August 1914*, observes: "Who is conceited enough to imagine that he can actually *devise* ideal institutions? The only people who think they can are those who believe that nothing significant was ever done before their own time, that their generation will be the first to achieve anything worthwhile, people who are convinced that only they and their current idols possess the truth, and that anyone who doesn't agree with them is a fool or a knave . . . ; it's a universal law—intolerance is the first sign of an inadequate education. An ill-educated person behaves with arrogant impatience, whereas truly profound education breeds humility." [1]

One of the curious anomalies of much contemporary thinking is the apparent belief that there is an irreconcilable conflict between learning on its higher levels and the education of the multitude. It is of course true that the same educational patterns are not suitable for all of humankind, something that a few theorists have not always conceded. But there is no reason why we cannot have the best of higher learning and the most suitable educational procedures for everyone able to benefit from them. If we could afford both guns and butter, we can afford both ivory towers and mass education. We must. But not all learned institutions must dispense the same intellectual and social nutriments to the populace.

The founding fathers of the nation were enormously concerned with the problems of education on various levels because they realized that the future stability of the govern-

[1] Alexander Solzhenitsyn, *August 1914*, trans. Michael Glenny (New York, 1972), p. 409.

ment would depend on the intelligence of its citizenry. The leaders, men of enlightenment and wisdom, were deeply conscious of their responsibilities. They had brought into being a republic, a new type of government in the modern world. Nothing like it had existed since the days of the Athenian democracy and the early Roman republic. They had to make certain that the republic did not perish. As we approach the celebration of the Bicentennial, we shall hear much about the founding fathers, and we can profitably spend a few moments now considering their views on learning and the social order. Fortunately, we have conveniently available two volumes of correspondence between Thomas Jefferson and John Adams in which these acute minds discuss, among other things, the quality of leadership required by the American republic and the kind of learning needed to produce men of "talent and virtue." Both Jefferson and Adams, steeped in the literature of Greece and Rome, looked back to the classical world for guidance. Indeed, the founding fathers drew heavily upon ancient writers for precedents in establishing our particular kind of constitutional government.

They found most useful, not theoretical philosophy, but the works of historians and writers on practical politics: Thucydides, Polybius, Tacitus, and Cicero. But, of Plato, Adams observed that the only useful thing he learned after laboriously going through the philosopher's works was that "sneezing is a cure for the hiccups." [2]

The classical historians, on the other hand, taught the founding fathers the necessity of an intelligent electorate if the republic was to survive. Ignorance would be the certain ruin of a democracy. They found in the survival of the Athenian democracy, which lasted longer than any democracy now extant (241 years),[3] proof of what a high level of cultural attainment would do. Although Rome's military might

[2] *The Adams-Jefferson Letters*, ed. Lester J. Cappon, 2 vols. (Chapel Hill, N.C., 1959), 2:437.

[3] Chester G. Starr, *The Ancient Greeks* (New York, 1971), p. 57.

ultimately conquered Greece, Greek culture conquered Rome.[4]

The hazard of ignorance to the mere survival of a republican form of government is vividly set forth in one of Adams's letters to Jefferson, dated July 13, 1813. The first time the two men disagreed on any fundamental point, Adams recalls, was when Jefferson expressed the opinion that the French Revolution would succeed "in establishing a free republican government." Adams was "well persuaded" that a country of 25,000,000 people of whom 24,500,000 "could neither write nor read" could no more govern itself than could the animals in the zoo at Versailles.[5] Leveling *down* to incorporate the ignorant multitude in the government would only result in anarchy.

Although Jefferson and Adams had often differed diametrically in their political views, they agreed that even in a republic such as they had brought to life, the rise of an aristocracy was inevitable and, indeed, desirable. Where they differed again was in the definition of the term and in the best methods of insuring a benevolent and virtuous aristocracy. They agreed that the encouragement of learning of the highest order was essential. The nation could not long guarantee good government, even freedom to its citizens, without a supply of wise leaders. These, Jefferson believed, would derive from what he called a "natural aristocracy," men possessed of "talent and virtue," who would emerge from a society that supplied a system of education in which the most talented would be constantly pushed to the top.

Adams was more skeptical. "The five pillars of aristocracy," he maintained, "are beauty, wealth, birth, genius, and virtues." [6] Although agreeing with Jefferson on many points, he did not believe that the new republic could hope to produce *only* a natural aristocracy of talented and virtuous men. The tradition of an aristocracy of birth and wealth was too well established in Virginia and New England, he declared.

[4] Ibid., p. 139.   [5] *Adams-Jefferson Letters* 2:355.
[6] Ibid., 2:371.

"Even in Rhode Island, where there has been no clergy, no church, and I had almost said no state, and some people say no religion, there has been a constant respect for certain old families." [7]

Both Jefferson and Adams agreed that ignorant demagoguery was a danger to the state. They had different views about their faith in the people. Jefferson was an optimist, Adams a pessimist. Jefferson would trust in education to insure wise and just leaders; Adams would provide the means of learning but would not put all his faith in it. He would see that the government had sufficient checks and balances to keep all classes in equilibrium.

Jefferson's rebuttal of his friend Adams's view is probably best expressed in a famous letter dated October 28, 1813, in which he remarked: "I agree with you that there is a natural aristocracy among men. The grounds of this are virtue and talents. . . . There is also an artificial aristocracy founded on wealth and birth, without either virtue or talents; for with these it would belong to the first class. The natural aristocracy I consider as the most precious gift of nature for the instruction, the trusts, and government of society. . . . May we not even say that that form of government is the best which provides most effectually for a pure selection of these natural *aristoi* into the offices of government?" [8]

Elsewhere Jefferson elaborated his theories about the kind of education needed in a republic governed by a natural aristocracy. As early as 1778 he drafted for the Virginia Assembly a "Bill for the More General Diffusion of Knowledge," which provided for three levels of education. Counties would be divided into manageable school "wards." All children would attend these ward schools, which would provide the essentials needed by every literate citizen. On completing the ward schools, the most promising children would then be selected to go on to district schools for further instruction. The best of the district schoolchildren would be winnowed out to proceed to the university for advanced learning, the

---

[7] Ibid., 2:400.   [8] Ibid., 2:388.

best they could absorb. From these would come the natural aristocracy, a body of men and women trained in both the sciences and letters, who would be the inevitable leaders in society. The Assembly declined to pass Jefferson's bill.

Again, in 1817, Jefferson drafted a "Bill for Establishing a System of Public Education," but once more the Assembly refused to act, because, Jefferson commented, the members "do not generally possess information enough to perceive the important truths that knowledge is power, that knowledge is safety, and that knowledge is happiness." [9] Having failed to persuade Virginia's legislators to provide the educational means to insure a natural aristocracy of talent and virtue, Jefferson set to work to create a university that would train a learned elite. The result was the University of Virginia, authorized by legislation on January 25, 1819. Jefferson designed the architecture of the new university, prescribed the curriculum, helped find the professors, and lived to see the first classes offered in 1825–26. He conceived of the university as an institution for the talented few, an institution for professional training in the highest reaches of the sciences and the humanities, which would be kept in a proper balance. This was the dream of a man who had no fear of creating an elite, the dream of the apostle of democracy. For Jefferson was a realist who believed that no state could flourish for long without an intelligent and learned leadership.

The need for institutions of genuine learning was critical, Jefferson believed. In a mood of discouragement over the superficiality of much education, and the ignorant arrogance of youth, Jefferson wrote Adams on July 5, 1814: "Our post-Revolutionary youth are born under happier stars than you and I were. They acquire all learning in their mothers' wombs, and bring it into the world ready made. The information of books is no longer necessary, and all knowledge which is not innate is in contempt or neglect at least. Every folly must run its round and so, I suppose, must that of self-

[9] Ibid., 2:478.

learning and self-sufficiency, of rejection of knowledge acquired in past ages. . . . [Petty academies are springing up in every neighborhood.] They commit their pupils to the theatre of the world with just taste enough of learning to be alienated from industrious pursuits and not enough to do service in the ranks of science. . . . I hope the necessity will at length be seen of establishing institutions, here as in Europe, where every branch of science, useful at this day, may be taught in its highest degrees." [10]

Jefferson's complaint about the rejection of traditional learning by the youth of his day might have been written yesterday, for the words sound strangely modern. This rejection in part resulted from doctrines disseminated by Jean Jacques Rousseau, doctrines that plague us still. Rousseau, who gained his first recognition in 1749 with an essay proclaiming the superiority of primitive society over civilization and the nobility of the savage, was the original alienated youth, dropout, and deadbeat. Previous to his prize-winning essay on the noble savage, he had been a failure at everything he had undertaken, a whining fellow who felt sorry for himself and spent his time cultivating his ego, all of which he later explained in boring detail in his *Confessions.*

A taste of literary success turned Rousseau into a copious author. His lachrymose and sentimental novel *La Nouvelle Héloïse* (1761) was an immense success. It was soon followed by *Le Contrat Social* (1762), for literary acclaim had now made Rousseau an authority on political science—a phenomenon not unknown in our time. In 1762 he also published *Émile,* a treatise on education in the guise of a novel. In this work Rousseau advocated complete permissiveness in dealing with pupils who would be guided by their own intuitions. Emotions would substitute for mentality.

Émile, too, had a great success, and its influence is still with us. Although Rousseau knew precisely how other parents ought to liberate their children, he solved his own problem by sending to a foundling home the five offspring born to him and Thérèse, a servant maid.

[10] Ibid., 2:434.

The impractical sentimentalities of Rousseau and his kind were too much for honest John Adams. In a letter to Jefferson on July 12, 1813, he commented: "I have never read reasoning more absurd, sophistry more gross in proof of the Athanasian creed or transubstantiation, than the subtle labors of Helvetius and Rousseau to demonstrate the equality of mankind." [11]

Although Rousseau's advocacy of permissiveness, his rejection of traditional learning, and his assertion of the emotions as the true guide of life won many converts, not everyone fell for his sentimental doctrines. Hardheaded thinkers looked back to an earlier tradition of orderly and disciplined education to produce leaders capable of guiding the state. Nevertheless, the controversy started in the eighteenth century by Rousseau's educational notions still rages today.

The educational theories advocated by thoughtful Americans in the early periods of our history had their origins in the Renaissance. In the late-fifteenth and sixteenth centuries Europeans rediscovered in the literature and art of Greece and Rome those civilizing values which we describe as humanism. In the words of a recent historian, Greek art "did not favor experimentation and breaking away from convention which we find in the arts today; the aim was rather to restrain and civilize the emotions." [12] Pericles insisted that reason must not be swept aside by the emotions. Thucydides attributed the Athenian disasters in the Peloponnesian War to the tendency of the people to be swayed by their emotions rather than by their minds. The equilibrium between mind and emotion, the golden mean between extremes, the quest for symmetry and perfection in both art and life, the belief in the attainment of certain universal verities, these were qualities that men of the Renaissance thought they saw in the classical world and sought to imitate. To this end the Renaissance glorified learning and made it fashionable. Furthermore, to the Renaissance profound learning was eminently practical. The men of that age did not regard scholarship as an escape from the world of affairs. Many of the

---

[11] Ibid., 2:355.   [12] Starr, *Ancient Greeks*, p. 129.

greatest artists and writers of the Renaissance were profound scholars who believed they had an obligation to utilize their learning for the good of the state.[13] This was an ideal that carried over into a later day and was transmitted to America in colonial times.

In sixteenth-century England, learning had an immense prestige and determined the careers of many men. The Tudor sovereigns, no mean scholars themselves, encouraged learning. Henry VII and Henry VIII both imported scholars from Italy to serve as historians, diplomats, counselors, and instructors in their courts. Queen Elizabeth I, who could deliver an impromptu speech in Latin when need arose, surrounded herself with a galaxy of brilliant men, noted for their learning as well as for their grace as courtiers. Few better examples of the well-rounded and talented "Renaissance man" could be found than Sir Philip Sidney, scholar, poet, critic, diplomat, and soldier. Learning was so fashionable that those who did not possess the needed background of scholarship depended upon convenient handbooks to get them over difficult hurdles. So strong was the tradition of scholarship that the British Foreign Office until very recently has held that an education in the classics provided the best background for a member of the diplomatic service.

One of Queen Elizabeth's own diplomats demonstrated his belief in learning in a very practical way. He founded what for many generations was the greatest research library in the English-speaking world. This man was Sir Thomas Bodley, who gave his name to the Bodleian Library at Oxford.

Bodley was an extraordinary man—a scholar and diplomat as well as a philanthropist.[14] Born in 1545 and living until 1613, he served Queen Elizabeth ably as an ambassador to Denmark, France, and the Low Countries. Learned in Hebrew and Greek, as a young man he lectured at Ox-

[13] For more detail on this subject, see Chapter VII, above.

[14] A portion of this material on Bodley is adapted from an article by Louis B. Wright, "Some Early 'Friends' of Libraries," *The Huntington Library Quarterly* 2 (1939):355–69.

ford. A contemporary of Shakespeare, he despised his fellow Elizabethan's craft and would not allow the library he founded at Oxford to harbor plays by Shakespeare or any of his contemporaries. Bodley was determined to gather only learned works useful to scholars—and modern plays, in his opinion, were trash. He could not foresee that three centuries later Elizabethan drama would also become the subject of learned research.

Although Bodley's ideas may seem to us a bit eccentric, they were consistent with the ideas of the time. A university library was a research library—not a place for the entertainment or even the elementary instruction of undergraduates. Hence Bodley would exclude works for which he could see no scholarly use.

In 1597, the very year in which other philanthropists were formulating a national plan for the relief of the poor, Bodley made an offer to the vice-chancellor of Oxford to restore the abandoned rooms formerly occupied by an earlier library left to the university by Humphrey, duke of Gloucester—a library scattered during the turmoil of the Reformation. Bodley's offer was accepted, and he set to work with dedication and singleness of purpose to establish the best research library the country had ever seen. He was not the kind of donor who would think a fine building made a library. Bodley concerned himself with the collection of books and manuscripts.

As a diplomat and public servant, he had some acquaintance with the leading figures of the day, and he bombarded them with requests for help, for donations of books or money. His success was phenomenal. Large gifts came from Lord Lumley, Lord Hunsdon, Lord Buckhurst, the bishop of Hereford, Sir Walter Raleigh, the earl of Essex, and many others. After Queen Elizabeth's death, in 1603, Bodley approached the new sovereign, James I, enlisted his interest, and procured a gift of the king's own works—a tactful move, for King James was vain of his own learning.

An amusing incident occurred a bit later, when King James came to inspect the new library. For weeks before the king's visit, Bodley wrote feverishly to his librarian, Thomas James, giving instructions designed to please the royal guest. Bodley was no blind worshiper of King James, but he had designs on a portion of the royal library. Because the king disliked long boring speeches, Bodley wrote his librarian to compose a speech in Latin that should be "short and sweet and full of stuff" and to pronounce the Latin in the King's Scottish manner. Because the vain monarch was certain to ask to see his own works, Bodley instructed his librarian to hide them and to say that the books had been sent out to be bound in fine velvet—but on no account to spend money for such a purpose. He was willing to flatter the king, but not to pay for binding works that he probably secretly despised.

In season and out, Bodley drove home the idea that learned works were needed, but he refused to accept what he called riff-raff books. In 1612 he wrote indignantly to the librarian about the cataloguing of a recent shipment of books from London. "There are many idle books, and riff-raffs among them," Bodley grumbled, "which shall never come into the library . . . almanacs, plays, and proclamations, of which I will have none but such as are singular." Two weeks later he again wrote protesting even more vehemently the addition to the library of "such books as almanacs, plays, and an infinite number that are daily printed of very unworthy matters."

Although Bodley spurned contemporary English literature that later generations would wish that he had preserved, he collected works in foreign languages if they seemed sufficiently scholarly. A university was the place for the highest studies, he insisted, and Oxford's scholars would know what to do with esoteric materials. When Lady Katherine Sandys in 1606 gave the library £20, Bodley bought eight volumes in Chinese. To Bodley—and to most Oxford dons—Chinese represented the uttermost reaches of erudition, and the founder was convinced that his library ought to have works in that tongue.

Interest in the Orient was stirred at this time by the activities of the Levant and East India companies. That fact may account for the zeal to accumulate books in oriental languages. In 1611, for instance, Bodley persuaded the English factor of the Levant Company at Aleppo to send a quantity of Persian, Arabic, and other manuscripts. Throughout the world, wherever Englishmen had gone, Bodley sent letters soliciting works that he believed would be useful some day to Oxford scholars.

To the end of his life, Bodley busied himself with the development of his library. In the year before his death he pawned his silver plate and borrowed money for his beloved institution. When his will was read, it revealed that he had left £7,000 to his foundation—a very large sum in those days. At this point perhaps we ought to pause a moment and give some credit to the rich widow whom Bodley had married, Mrs. Anne Ball, from whose estate much of Bodley's money came. So far as I know, I am the only person who has ever mentioned Mrs. Ball in gratitude. Bodley's relatives were disappointed and complained about being left out of his will. A gossip of the day wrote that Bodley "was so carried away with the vanity and vainglory of his library that he forgot all other respects and duties almost."

Whatever his motives, the singleness of purpose displayed by Bodley enabled him to create the finest and most enduring monument any man could have. But his foundation has been more than that. The influence of the Bodleian Library upon the minds and spirits of scholars for more than three centuries has been immeasurable. The momentum that the founder gave to this great research institution kept it going through the centuries, and its influence has been international in scope.

In Bodley's time—as in ours—heavy pressure was exerted upon philanthropists to contribute to humanitarian causes. In 1597 the unemployed of England were crying for bread; the sick were suffering for lack of hospitals; widows and orphans were destitute. Bodley was criticized because he turned a deaf ear to appeals for charitable donations. He might have concerned himself with public welfare and helped out with donations to the unemployed. If he had, a trifling number would have called him blessed but the good that he did would have been interred with his bones.

To Bodley there was a higher service to the state than caring for a few broken bodies that would soon be dust. The preservation of the living thought of great men who had gone before, and the transmission of that thought to future generations, seemed to Bodley more important than making easier the hard lot of widows and orphans or giving a few crusts to the poor. Measured in sentimental terms, Bodley was a hard man, as some of his acquaintances said. But if he had not given all his energy and means to the collection and preservation of books—objects that must have seemed inanimate and dead to unthinking sentimentalists—our civilization would have lost a potent influence that has made it better and finer.

I have dwelt on Bodley's benefaction because it illustrates the kind of institution that is sometimes described as an ivory tower divorced from the needs of the world, a warehouse of dusty tomes. Much of my own career has been concerned with such institutions, and I can testify to their utility to society. Institutions of this type, be they libraries or scientific foundations, are essential if we are to survive as a nation of intelligent men and women. It is a grave mistake to expect them to devote their energies and their means to problems of immediate social utility. Yet that precisely is what the unlearned and unthinking public has been demanding—and that "public" may include trustees who ought to know better.

My scientific colleagues in the Cosmos Club, I feel certain, could furnish dramatic illustrations of the value of laboratories and scientific institutes devoted to so-called pure research—as if some research should be classified as "impure." In the long sweep of time much of the speculative thinking by scientists, which appeared to have no applied utility at the moment, has contributed to fundamental discoveries that have changed the world. It has become a commonplace to cite the abstract theories of Albert Einstein as a case in point. For Einstein was not devoting himself to applied science. He was thinking. His most recent biographer observes: "In late summer of 1933 he went back to England, staying in relative isolation in Cromer and happily losing count of the days as he worked on his calculations. He was soon to say that the ideal job for a theoretical physicist would be that of a lighthouse keeper." [15] In some respects, a lighthouse would be better than an ivory tower.

But why belabor the point that society must maintain learned institutions not concerned with immediate social utility? That fact ought to be obvious to any intelligent citizen. The necessity arises because of a curious either-or philosophy that is widespread today. Either you are out doing good in the streets, or you are failing in your obligation to the underprivileged. Let me quote another passage from Solzhenitsyn's novel, *August 1914*. A student asks the question: "But can't a soul be saved in the very process of sacrificing itself for the people?" And the reply is: "But what if that sacrifice proves to have been misconceived? Don't people have any *obligations*? Or do they have only *rights*? Are they simply meant to sit and wait while we first supply them with happiness, then provide for their 'eternal interests'? And what if the people themselves aren't ready? Because if they aren't, then neither food nor education nor a change of institutions will be of any use." If this be heretical doctrine in Russia, it is equally distasteful to many do-gooders among us. Either we must sacrifice abstract learning and nonutilitarian science to the present welfare of the multitude, or we demonstrate a callous lack of compassion.

You will say such a view is illogical and nonsensical, and it is, but it is a current hazard to learning. It is true that the Bodleian Library, the Cavendish Laboratories, the Institute for Advanced Study, and scores of other learned institutions on both sides of the Atlantic have no vocation for charitable enterprises, but an incredible number of people have convinced themselves that everybody "in these times" ought to bestir himself to become his brother's keeper.

[15] Banesh Hoffman and Helen Dukas, *Albert Einstein, Creator and Rebel* (New York, 1972), p. 170.

During the past decade we were the victims of a wave of virulent antiintellectualism which glorified the primitivism of Rousseau, added a touch of ill-understood Freudianism, and substituted the emotions for the mind. Nobody was guilty of anything; only society was to blame for any individual's crime. The legacy of Western civilization was evil and responsible for an oppressive Establishment, which would have to be wiped out to insure an era of love and equality. This new dispensation preferred Timbuktu to Athens.

Fortunately the tide has turned, and no longer are vandals burning down college and university buildings, destroying library collections, holding deans and college presidents as hostages, and otherwise demonstrating their demand for "relevance" and freedom from bondage to Western culture.

But the turmoil within academia and the demand outside for correction of the ills of society explain in part the pressures upon all types of institutions, regardless of their fitness, to "do something" for the public good. To meet this demand, institutions have sometimes been obliged to squander meager financial resources and sacrifice energies needed for their primary tasks. In so doing they are selling their institutions short. Scholars and scientists serve society best by sticking to their lasts, by doing what they are best fitted to do.

An interview with scholars in Cambridge, Massachusetts, published in the *Washington Post* on February 18, 1973, is entitled "Scholars Examine Value of Social Scientists in Public Policy." The scholars interviewed seemed to conclude that social scientists had been of doubtful benefit in the public arena. Adam Yarmolinsky, now a professor at the University of Massachusetts and for a period deputy director of a presidential task force dealing with the war on poverty, is quoted as saying: "Perhaps today's scholar needs to learn to keep his distance, too, from the world of action, or at least to plot periodic strategic retreats in order to regain his perspective." The ivory tower—or Einstein's lighthouse—thus has a practical utility as a retreat for scholars who need to think and reorient themselves.

If the individual scholar, with a few notable exceptions, is of doubtful value in the implementing and the conduct of public affairs, as the foregoing interviews imply, the learned institution has even less aptitude for meddling where it has no skill. In such endeavors it will usually waste its resources to no purpose.

Never in our history have we had so great a need for men and women of brains and character, for the United States, somewhat unwillingly, has been obliged to assume a leadership in the world for which it was not adequately prepared. Our universities and learned institutions—all ivory towers in the popular conception—have a tremendous obligation to provide a supply of leaders possessed of wisdom. Our very existence may depend upon the quality of the leadership we produce. We particularly need to induce a sense of perspective so that we will not be swept away by ephemeral influences. To that end a knowledge of history, which we too often lack, is essential.

Recent historic developments have thrust us into a strategic position between eastern Europe and Asia. We may find ourselves the balance wheel that must maintain the equilibrium of a peaceful world. We also have critical obligations in the Western Hemisphere, especially in Latin America. To provide our statesmen, diplomats, and technicians with all the knowledge available about the backgrounds and customs of the lands with which we must deal will be the responsibility of professional historians. The historian will have an imperative duty to be objective, for to be otherwise could lead to disaster. Of late some historians have turned advocate, but that makes of history mere propaganda. Advocacy of any cause is not the proper role for a legitimate historian. His duty is to provide description, explanation, and interpretation without prejudice. The historian will have an important influence in producing those natural aristocrats that Jefferson described. Jefferson did not expect scholars and teachers to abandon their classrooms for the fray of public life. Their job was to train leaders.

In an address on the occasion of the Second Cosmos Club Award, my friend and colleague of long standing, Dr. Henry

Allen Moe, spoke "On the Need for an Aristocracy." His definition of an aristocracy was essentially the same as Jefferson's. Like Jefferson, Dr. Moe took an optimistic view of society. He commented: "My thesis is that we have a better chance than any people ever had to maintain an aristocracy of brains and character." He thought that opportunity derives not from leveling down in our educational processes but from leveling up to produce "an aristocracy with a conscience and taste and a sense of history."

Despite brainless attacks on learning, which have also occurred from time to time in previous ages, we in America have unparalleled opportunities for the cultivation of the mind and the spirit on the highest levels. Philanthropists have poured out their treasure to encourage research. No region lacks facilities for advanced scholarship in science and the humanities. We have innumerable towers of strength from which the competent may get a better vision of the world and the perspective required to guide others. But we must not squander and dissipate these opportunities by pressuring learned institutions to diffuse their energies and resources in miscellaneous "good works." Their obligation is to provide an incentive to excellence and that vision without which the people perish.

XI

The Obligation of Intellectuals to Be Intelligent: Some Commentary from Jefferson and Adams

IT IS FITTING that we stop today, the birthday of the nation and the death day of two of its chief architects, Thomas Jefferson and John Adams, to recall their dreams and aspirations for the republic that they had helped to bring to life. Both were concerned about the kind of men and women who would perpetuate the traditions they had sought to establish, and, as a consequence, they were profoundly interested in the process of education. They differed in their political philosophies, but they had been friends and colleagues in the struggle for independence; and, reconciled in their old age to their differences, they carried on a fascinating epistolary discussion of the problems of society. It is some of their commentary on learning that I want to discuss in a moment.

In approaching so important a theme in these troublous times, one might expect a text from Marcus Aurelius—or, perhaps, Jeremiah. Instead, I want to quote a few observations from a more recent philosopher, a baseball genius whom some of you may remember, one Leroy Paige, commonly known as Old Satch. In a little broadside that lately came into my hands, Satch provides some practical advice on meeting the vicissitudes of life, and I quote from the remarks attributed to him: "(1) Avoid fried foods which angry up the blood. (2) If your stomach disputes you, lie down and pacify it with cool thoughts. (3) Keep the juices flowing by jangling around gently as you move. (4) Go very lightly on the vices, such as carrying on in society. The social ramble ain't restful. (5) Avoid running at all times. (6) Don't look back. Something may be gaining on you."

Future historians may find in Satch's formula significant clues to the preoccupations of our times. His last point, especially, emphasizes a current apprehension: "Don't look back. Something may be gaining on you."

Many of our prominent social thinkers today are not looking back, either afraid that something untoward might overtake us or convinced that there is nothing back there worthy of their intellectual response. The cynics are fearful that barbarism is approaching at a gallop; certain "advanced thinkers" have convinced themselves that there is nothing to be learned from looking backward to historical precedents. This was not the view of Jefferson, an idealist with faith in the innate intelligence of the common man, nor of Adams, a realist with less trust in the mass of the populace. They both believed that in the wisdom of the ancients Americans had much to learn. This, I realize, is now heresy to many who feel certain that all wisdom derives from "innovative" processes, but I trust you will forgive me if I cite the antiquated beliefs of two of the founding fathers who did not have the benefit of recent doctrines of bright young minds in our better universities.

Jefferson's idealism of course stirred his political enemies to accuse him of impracticality and inability to understand the problems of what today we would call the real world. But few men have held so consistently to idealistic beliefs throughout their lives and yet adapted to the compelling necessities of their times. Jefferson exemplified the Emersonian dictum that a foolish consistency is the hobgoblin of little minds. He believed that an intellectual had an obligation to be intelligent. If that sounds like a platitude, observers of academia-in-debate know better; they have frequently been depressed by the way some of their supposedly learned brethren react like Pavlov's dogs to outworn clichés that they treasure in their hearts as inherited dogma from Holy Writ.

One instance of Jefferson's adaptation of idealism to reality was his recognition that war with England in 1812 could not be avoided without jeopardizing the future of the United States. He wrote to Charles Pinckney on February 2, 1812: "We are to have war then? I believe so, and that it is necessary. Every hope from time, patience, and the love of peace is exhausted, and war or abject submission are the only alternative left us. I am forced from my hobby, peace." [1] Throughout his last administration he had struggled—by diplomacy and economic sanctions, even his unpopular embargo—to avoid war. Now he approved of President Madison's decision.

Jefferson and Madison, lifelong friends, had long debated many issues; and Madison, often more realistic than his friend, served as an acute and sometimes severe critic of some of Jefferson's idealistic theories. One significant fact ought to be remembered about their differing views: always they carried on their debates with courtesy and good humor. The intellectual in Jefferson's time felt that he had an obligation not only to listen intelligently, but always to have good manners.

In a famous exchange of views between Jefferson and Madison, resulting from a letter that Jefferson composed in Paris on September 6, 1789, but did not send until January 9, 1790, Jefferson set forth his oft-repeated doctrine that "the earth belongs always to the living generation." He would provide by law some way for the living always to have a portion of the earth and not permit men to devise ways of controlling it after their deaths. He also insisted that one generation had no right to force its debts on the next one, a condition that would limit the public debt to what each generation could pay. An accumulating public debt, increasing generation after generation, was to Jefferson unthinkable.

Madison disagreed with many of Jefferson's views, including this one. Tactfully, he based his reasons on the ground of "impracticality." Madison thus was useful as a critic of some of Jefferson's pet theories, and Jefferson accepted his comments with gracious reserve. "Nowhere in the friendship of fifty years," observes Adrienne Koch, "can we find a better expression of intellectual reciprocity. . . . The perfect courtesy that pervaded this and other intellectual en-

[1] Quoted in Bernard Mayo, *Jefferson Himself* (1942; reprint ed., Charlottesville, Va., 1970), p. 304.

145

counters made it possible for stringent criticism to be received without injury of pride." [2]

Jefferson, intellectual and idealist, realized that the welfare of the state often required the subordination of theoretical good to the practically possible. In his first inaugural address, March 4, 1801—after one of the dirtiest and most vicious campaign attacks upon him the country has yet witnessed (the source, incidentally, of some of the popular slander of Jefferson in a recent biography)—the new president declared that "all will, of course, arrange themselves under the will of the law and unite in common efforts for the common good. All, too, will bear in mind this sacred principle, that though the will of the majority is in all cases to prevail, that will, to be rightful, must be reasonable; that the minority possess their equal rights, which equal laws must protect, and to violate which would be oppression." Whatever theoretically and intellectually he might have wished, during the next eight years he put the good of the country ahead of his theories. The intellectual bowed to the necessity of being practically intelligent.

An example of the president's good sense is expressed in a letter he wrote to Dr. Walter Jones on March 31, 1801: "I am sensible how far I should fall short of effecting all the reformation which reason would suggest and experience approve, were I free to do whatever I thought best; but when we reflect how difficult it is to move or inflect the great machine of society, how impossible to advance the notions of a whole people suddenly to ideal right, we see the wisdom of Solon's remark that no more must be attempted than the nation can bear, and that all [we can do] will be chiefly to reform the waste of public money and thus drive away the vultures who prey upon it, and improve some little on old routines." [3] Advocate of revolution though he was, Jefferson would have found beyond his comprehension the vision of

[2] Adrienne Koch, *Jefferson and Madison: The Great Collaboration* (New York, 1950), p. 63.

[3] Quoted in Mayo, *Jefferson Himself*, p. 226.

college professors leading a mindless mob intent upon burning down ROTC buildings—and even libraries—to show their displeasure over some action of the government.

Jefferson's views on education have been so often discussed that they do not need detailed iteration here, but perhaps we ought to remember that although he created a university devoted to the highest ideals of research and scholarship, he never once thought of learning as mere social decoration. Although he believed that the welfare of the nation depended on the development of an educated leadership, an intellectual elite or aristocracy of intelligence, he would have been horrified at the notion of the academic community preening itself upon its superiority merely because it had acquired the statutory awards of advanced degrees. True learning, he believed, induced intellectual humility—a quality that he himself exemplified.

The correspondence between Jefferson and Adams after they had both retired from the heat of political battles is an extraordinary reservoir of wisdom on the theme of learning and its utility to society. These two wise founding fathers might have differed on many points, but they agreed that the nation somehow had to insure an adequate supply of leaders whose learning was equal to their responsibilities. That did not mean "intellectuals" who paraded their erudition to no purpose, who pretended to omniscience because they had acquired some proficiency in a special field. Constantly in their letters both Jefferson and Adams expressed their dislike of windy rhetoric, the pomposity of pedants, and intellectual pretentiousness.

Learning without substance, knowledge without utility to society, speculative philosophy that led only to finespun arguments that delighted the philosophers and their sycophants, both men deplored. Jefferson wrote Adams on January 21, 1812, that the much-vaunted education of France and England had succeeded only in making a den of robbers of one and a nest of pirates of the other. If learning could do no better than that, he would "rather wish our country to be ignorant, honest, and estimable as our neighboring savages are." [4] And he added: "I have given up newspapers in exchange for Tacitus and Thucydides, for Newton and Euclid; and I find myself much happier." In a reply dated February 3, 1812, Adams commented: "What an exchange you have made! Of newspapers for Newton! Rising from the lower deep of the lowest deep of dullness and bathos to the contemplation of the heavens and the heaven of heavens." And he expressed regret that he had wasted so much of his own time on useless reading and writers of no value to him or society.

Foggy philosophers received utter damnation from both Adams and Jefferson. Indeed, Jefferson was inclined to blame deficiencies in modern education on professorial adherence to philosophic doctrines that they ill understood. In a letter to Adams dated July 5, 1814, discussing, among other things, Plato's *Republic* and his bewilderment at the continuing influence of so muddy a mind, he observed: "With the moderns, I think, it is rather a matter of fashion and authority. Education is chiefly in the hands of persons who, from their profession, have an interest in the reputation and dreams of Plato. They give the tone while at school, and few, in their after-years, have occasion to revise their college opinions." As so often in his observations about education, Jefferson hit upon one of the conditions that never change. Substitute Marcuse or Marx or any guru of the Left or the Right who happens to find a following and become fashionable among young intellectuals in our colleges and universities, and you have the educational condition that Jefferson complained of. Youthful academics like to exhibit their fashionable philosophies, however weird, to their classes. Sometimes, alas, they grow old in their ignorance and never lapse into intelligence. This was the problem that troubled Jefferson and Adams.

Among fashionable philosophers, ancient and modern, the two who found least favor in the eyes of both Adams and

[4] Quotations from the letters of Adams and Jefferson unless otherwise indicated, are from *The Adams-Jefferson Letters*, ed. Lester J. Cappon, 2 vols. (Chapel Hill, N.C., 1959).

Jefferson were Plato and Rousseau. Elsewhere I have mentioned this point, and if my remarks sound like a sequel to something I have written before, they are so intended.[5] The reasons for this distaste on the part of Adams and Jefferson have a modern "relevance," if I may be forgiven the use of that hackneyed bit of jargon beloved of reformers. Both men were convinced that neither Plato nor Rousseau exhibited any intelligent comprehension of society as it existed, or even as it might become.

In a reply to Jefferson's letter on the subject, Adams, on July 16, 1814, expressed in detail his own puzzlement over Rousseau, Plato, and other philosophers, and concluded cynically: "In short, philosophers, ancient and modern, appear to me as mad as Hindus, Mohammedans, and Christians. No doubt they would all think me mad; and for anything I know this globe may be the bedlam . . . of the universe." It should be explained that the two men had previously discussed the way religion, especially Christianity, had in their opinions been perverted because simple and pure doctrines had been engrafted with philosophic interpretations that had led to controversy, persecution, and bloodshed.

Jefferson had also expressed his disappointment over the inadequacies of education as he observed it; he wondered at the sublime conviction of youth that they "acquire all learning in their mothers' womb[s] and bring it into the world ready-made." The kind of education that many of them received served only to confirm them in the arrogance of ignorance. Had he lived to the present day, he would have had reason for greater gloom, for vocal educational theorists have certified that secondary schoolchildren have the innate competence, clearly brought with them into the world, to choose what subjects they should study—and even to sit on boards that prescribe curricula. All in all, Jefferson and Adams deplored intellectuals, educationists, and theorists who never deviated into sense.

Good manners, these men believed, were also a mark of

[5] See Chapter X, above.

intelligence. The intellectual, because he was presumably also intelligent, would display good manners with his fellow beings. In a letter to Dr. Benjamin Rush dated January 3, 1808, telling him that he was sending his grandson, Thomas Jefferson Randolph, to Philadelphia to be educated, Jefferson expressed the hope that the youth possessed "what I value more than all things, good humor," for good humor also implied good manners. "For thus I estimate the qualities of the mind," he added, "1, good humor; 2, integrity; 3, industry; 4, science [meaning knowledge]." We would all prefer to associate with a good-humored personality with good manners, he explained, than with "an ill-tempered rigorist in morality." [6]

In a letter to this grandson, following the letter to Dr. Rush, Jefferson elaborated on the value of good humor and good manners: "I have mentioned good humor as one of the preservatives of our peace and tranquillity. It is among the most effectual [qualities] . . . and its effect is . . . aided artificially by politeness, that this also becomes an acquisition of first-rate value. In truth, politeness is artificial good humor; it covers the natural want of it and ends by rendering habitual a substitute nearly equivalent to the real virtue. . . . How cheap a price for the good will of another." He also warned against arguments and disputes, because "I never saw an instance of one or two disputants convincing the other by argument. . . . It was one of the rules, which above all others, made Doctor Franklin the most amiable of men in society, 'Never to contradict anybody.' If he was urged to announce an opinion, he did it rather by asking questions, as if for information, or by suggesting doubts." [7]

Jefferson and his contemporaries—Franklin, Adams, Madison, and scores of others—put a high premium on good manners, even in the heat of political controversy. They realized that good manners served as a social lubricant—and often resulted in winning a point that might otherwise have been dissipated by rudeness. In youth, they insisted, good man-

[6] Mayo, *Jefferson Himself*, p. 272.
[7] Letter dated November 24, 1808, quoted in ibid., pp. 272–73.

ners were a sine qua non. A rude young man placed himself beyond the pale. No justification of "sincerity" or other reason, however valid, excused improper behavior.

Rudeness among educated men was equally intolerable. From the great writers of antiquity and from the Renaissance, they had received lessons on the importance of courtesy as one of the cardinal virtues. Educated men in the days of Adams and Jefferson were a society of gentlemen.

I do not need to embroider this theme any longer. I merely want to repeat that our age has much to learn from these two wise men. When John Adams died, on July 4, 1826, his last words were: "Thomas Jefferson still lives." He was right, though Jefferson's earthly life had ended just a few hours before Adams's on the same day. Jefferson does still live, in this place and in the hearts and minds of thoughtful men, as does his great friend and sometime political antagonist, John Adams.